The Experts Welcome **Business-to-Business Marketing:**
Creating a Community of Customers

There is a small roster of leaders who created and nurtured the concept of business-to-business marketing. Vic Hunter is one of these early champions. Whether through his seminars or through this new book, he has used his passion for the customer to help each of us create better marketing strategies, more successful business plans, more inclusive sales opportunities. He knows how to drive us past the thinking stage into taking action. *He is a fire-starter.*

Marilyn Rutland, Vice President, U.S. Dental Division
Henry Schein, Inc.

This book is revolutionary. I'm convinced Vic Hunter and his associates have set the standard for business-to-business marketing in the 21st century.

Bob Stone, Chairman Emeritus
Stone & Adler, Inc.

What an exceptional book! While many marketers are still trying to tweak old sales and marketing paradigms, Vic Hunter has a realistic vision of how companies must change their approach in order to remain competitive in today's tough business environment. Truly innovative thinking and a must read for any executive responsible for his or her company's future marketing plans.

Chuck Tannen, President
Target Conference Corporation

The ground rules in business-to-business marketing have definitely changed. No longer is it market share, or return on sales and assets. The goal now is not just selling the product, but owning the customer relationship. A "Community of Customers" is the company's single greatest asset.

> **Rick Keane, CBC, Executive Director**
> **Business Marketing Association**

At last . . . a book that translates consumer service ideas into a business-to-business setting. Hunter and Tietyen have written a "must read" implementation guide for business marketers!

> **Leonard A. Schlesinger**
> **George F. Baker, Jr., Professor of Business Administration**
> **Harvard University**

Vic Hunter's approach to marketing is unique, creative and sales enhancing. I appreciated his insight during our years together working with Amoco TBA.

> **Dan Beers, Director, Partner Development**
> **Amoco Oil Company**

Vic Hunter's methodology proved relevant to every department at GTSI. We expect this methodology to become an important factor as we reengineer our company for success.

> **M. Dendy Young, President and CEO**
> **GTSI**

Two types of pioneers can alter the norms of how commerce succeeds in America: those who discover a better way and those who put that better way into practice. Vic Hunter is one of the unique breed of entrepreneurs who meets both aspects of that definition. He has refined the art of database marketing and put it to use in solidifying business relationships.

Edward L. Schmitz, Director,
New Business Development
Shell Oil Products Company

If you want to rethink your whole concept of "customer marketing," you won't do better than to start with Hunter and Tietyen . . . their thinking is 10 years ahead of anyone else's. . . . Practical . . . Solid . . . Intelligent . . . and born out of frontline experience, not back-end theories.

Donald R. Libey, Libey Incorporated
Direct marketing futurist, consultant, author, and speaker

Vic Hunter and his team have worked with us for six years. We used these concepts to build a strategic advantage in the marketplace and a productive Customer Service Center. Hunter Business Direct was a seamless extension of our field sales force. This book shares how to build that advantage into the business-to-business marketplace.

Tom Scott, Vice President
Toshiba America Information Systems

This is *an important book* for those companies wanting to become more customer-focused. Congratulations for hitting the target with your idea of "creating a community of customers." I have seen books treating parts of this subject matter, but never *all these great ideas and methods in one book*. Hunter's business-to-business model of customer relationship management is *unique* and very applicable.

Jon Anton, Professor, Center for Customer-Driven Quality Purdue University

At Hallmark Cards, Inc., a strong corporation and brand identity have both been built around the concept of enhancing personal relationships. In some respects Vic Hunter's customer-focused marketing strategy is an extension of that same philosophy into the workplace and marketing environment. That's why it was easy to embrace these concepts into Hallmark's new business-to-business initiatives. Although the organizational integration of such concepts remains challenging, Vic offers some *concrete examples* of how to begin implementing such a strategy. The customer community concept is compelling enough to withstand the necessary changes that need to ensue within the organization because, very simply put, *it works*.

Claire Brand, General Manager
Hallmark Business Expressions

Vic Hunter is one of the most thoughtful and experienced people involved in business-to-business marketing. He knows how to build a successful activity and his ideas are well worth considering.

Robert D. Kestnbaum, President
Kestnbaum & Company

I believe this book will be a major success. Vic Hunter does an outstanding job of explaining that in order to remain competitive, manufacturers need to understand the importance of becoming customer focused.

Hunter makes it very clear that integrated win-win interdependent strategic relationships with channel partners and customers are critical ingredients that will result in increased customer loyalty and sustainable profitable growth.

George S. Aalto, National Sales Manager
3M Dental Products Division

For the 29 years that I have been assisting business-to-business mail order marketing firms, my opening remarks to these clients have been "the secret to success in direct mail marketing is the proper utilization of the customer file." Vic Hunter and Dave Tietyen's in-depth book effectively covers this very broad area, which is vital and central to the ultimate success of any company in (direct) marketing.

Congratulations on a job well done.

Robert Foehl, President
Direct Media

In a highly competitive global marketplace, this idea of "creating a community of customers" is truly an intriguing and insightful way to do business—both short- and long-term.

Dr. Stephen R. Covey

BUSINESS
TO
BUSINESS
Marketing

BUSINESS
TO
BUSINESS
Marketing
CREATING
A COMMUNITY OF
CUSTOMERS

VICTOR L. HUNTER
WITH DAVID TIETYEN

NTC Business Books
NTC/Contemporary Publishing Company • Lincolnwood, Illinois USA

Library of Congress Cataloging-in-Publication Data

Hunter, Victor L., 1947–
    Business-to-business marketing: creating a community of
customers / Victor L. Hunter and David E. Tietyen.
      p.   cm.
    Includes bibliography/reference and index.
    ISBN 0-8442-3230-0 (alk. paper)
    1. Industrial marketing.   I. Tietyen, David   II. Title.
HF5415.1263.H86   1997
658.8$'$4—dc21
                                      96-40854
                                         CIP

10   9   8   7   6   5   4   3   2   1

*To my family—where community begins.
Especially to Linda my wife, and Holly,
Matt, Drew, and Jed who have taught me
the most about community.*

CONTENTS

FOREWORD

BY DICK ALBERDING
Executive Vice President (Retired)
Hewlett-Packard Company

Getting close to the customer has become one of the loudest rallying cries for doing business in the '90s. It follows that we've seen all types of new management techniques emerge, such as one-on-one marketing, relationship marketing, integrated marketing communication, and others. Even TQM and the once-popular "re-engineering" have built on internal and external customer relationships.

While all offer some promise, none take a total, or holistic, approach. Rather, they address only some of the issues of building long-term customer relationships without exploring the interdependencies that are critical for success. That's what sets apart the principles and practices described in this book—creating a community of customers through building interdependent relationships.

This is not just theory, it's a practical, economically viable approach that builds lasting customer relationships which reduce the costs of sales and marketing, and improve profits.

I know. In today's business vernacular, I've "been there... done that." In the mid-1980s, while I was responsible for worldwide marketing, sales, and support at Hewlett-Packard (HP), we began putting together a similar integrated marketing strategy that enabled HP to move from primarily a technology-driven company to one that was more market/customer driven. I can frankly say that I believe a significant part of HP's success in the past ten years has been related to using the integrated approach described in this book to build customer relationships.

Here are a few facts to support my case. When HP first became involved with Vic Hunter and his group, we had started to experience operating profit degradation. As a result, one of the key goals we set was to increase the productivity for all our sales channels by 15 percent. For us, a 15 percent worldwide increase in sales channel productivity was a formidable task. This was especially true when one considered we had noticeable weakness in our then product family, a soft worldwide economy, a company culture that didn't fire people (i.e., the HP Way), a direct sales force mentality with thousands of salespeople, an inefficient product generation process, an engineering-minded management, and finally a company moving from its test and measurement origin to that of an integrated *computer and instrumentation company.*

When we began working with Vic Hunter, we were initially interested in having Vic's group put together a direct mail program for us. However, it quickly became apparent that integrating phone, direct mail, and field sales contact would help dramatically increase both direct sales channel productivity as well as alternate, third-party channels that were fast expanding.

This naturally led to exploring the type of information that would be communicated through the mail and phone. When trying to answer this, we began to recognize that we did not have a good handle on our customers' needs. In fact, we found that too often we were developing products without a direct link to the customer.

This book documents what you need to do to understand your customer and use that understanding to build successful, sustainable business relationships and more successful products. It gives the practices to follow for determining how the customer perceives you, what the customer values in your relationship, how the customer wants to be contacted and about what, and how to build lasting customer relationships.

Most of the companies I know today have a strategy to offer differentiated products and/or solutions. Yet, I see companies drifting toward commodities, with little product differentiation. Perhaps this is an outcome of the galloping technological advances that are so prevalent today. However, I believe the way in which you differentiate yourself is through how you relate to your customer base. By focusing on, and then satisfying, the individual needs of the customer, one can gain a huge competitive advantage. Successful companies will be those with the ability to surround the customer with a warm security blanket through differentiated relationships.

Making the change from being product focused to being customer focused requires a different way to look at customers. A customer is not an account, but an individual. Only when you start treating customers as individuals can you begin the journey to a customer community, remove the barriers to communication, and make it easier for the customer to do business with you.

This is the essence of building a community of customers. You build value into the relationship by providing something of value with every customer contact. This builds an interdependence based on your ability to address a customer's unique needs. To achieve this, you need to understand your customer's business applications. Then, identify the value-based communications around the business applications within given market segments. Finally, you will discover a common set of needs around each business application, which in turn enables you to identify the value-based contacts for each.

The book you are about to read describes each step in this process. It shows you how to effectively, and cost-efficiently, integrate communication tools to ensure your customer receives value through each contact.

The principles and techniques discussed in this book work. Today they have become a part of the HP philosophy of doing business. They've become a part of the company's culture. And they can work for you—whether you are a multibillion dollar company or one at the other end of the spectrum. This fundamental approach works for any size business-to-business marketer. The principles are universal. They will enable you to truly get closer to your customer and win big!

ACKNOWLEDGMENTS

Many people contributed to the ideas and examples presented in this book and many provided encouragement and support. If we have inadvertently left anyone out, it was not intentional. We offer our deep-felt appreciation to the following:

First are our clients who have become a part of our community and were willing to share their stories in this book. It is their real-life struggles to bond with their customers that have proven most valuable in our learning.

One who believed in this book and was encouraging at every step of the process is Bob Stone. He was also instrumental in leading us to Rich Hagle at NTC, who immersed himself totally in this project, far beyond what one would expect from an editor.

Next is the community of Hunter Business Direct. They live the concepts each day. It is through their work that we have seen this value of interdependency economically forced in the marketplace. Special thanks to those who shared their experiences and knowledge including Mike McIntyre, Mark Peck, Jim Kurtz, Nick Poulos, and Kim Albrecht. Billie Fox and Jim Schoemer helped with the illustrations and graphics. And thanks to Arline Bloom, who became involved in all facets of the book.

Tim DeJarnette of Toshiba was instrumental in providing his insights and experience with the process of community building. And our longtime ally, Dick Alberding, was one of the earlier believers that this approach to business-to-business marketing was the future.

During the research phase, the library staff at the Milwaukee School of Engineering was extremely helpful and we thank them all.

Special thanks to our friends and families who were always encouraging. Especially to Yvonne, who had to cope with the erratic hours one puts in when writing and meeting deadlines and never complained. And to the Hunter family, who had to endure listening to chapters being read during miles of vacation driving.

1

A NEW MARKETING VISION

Not long ago, United Airlines aired a commercial that illustrated how dramatically the world of business has changed. It showed a grim-faced CEO announcing to a group of executives that they had lost a major account. He blamed the loss on the impersonalization of the business process. That's easy to understand. "Normal" ways of doing business can depersonalize the communication process. At the end of the commercial he pulled out a packet of airline tickets and announced that each executive was leaving to go out and personally visit the company's customers. He wanted to get back to the basics of quality marketing and selling—personal contact with the customer.

At one level, the commercial vividly illustrates the obvious importance of staying close to your customer. If you don't, you risk losing the business. At another level, it speaks to the

radical changes taking place in the business-to-business marketplace. If you are not seeing these, maybe it's time you took
another look.

During most of the 1980s, good products could literally sell
themselves. Companies focused on technological advances and
manufacturing efficiencies to produce profits. Emphasis was
placed on such techniques as total quality management, concurrent engineering, and cross-functional teams to bring better products to the market in less time. Fortunately, demand
outpaced supply in many product categories.

This has changed.

Increasing global competition, escalating technological
advances, and new buyer-seller arrangements are changing
how companies conduct business. And a new style of marketing is mandatory. Philip Kotler, whose textbook, *Marketing
Management,* is a staple at most business schools, commented
that the 4Ps of marketing are no longer valid: "We're on the
threshold of a new marketing paradigm. The simple 'Four Ps:
product, place, price and promotion' has become wrong for the
1990s. . . ."[1]

THE NEED FOR A NEW WAY OF DOING BUSINESS

Pick up any business magazine or book and you will find an
array of new terms, nostrums, and formulas for success in the
new business world that is emerging today. Many of these
"magic potions" are open to debate, but three trends that are
shaping the business world are unmistakable.

The first is companies are beginning to realize each
customer's needs are unique. That is, each customer has a

different problem, an "individual problem," to solve. Even companies in the same industry that superficially have the same, or very similar, profiles often operate under very different circumstances that influence how they do business and how they decide whom to do business with. And anyone selling successfully to these companies needs to be aware of these differences.

The second trend, which has grown out of the first, is the movement toward demassification. It has grown from the realization that individual people, not organizations, make decisions to buy. These decisions are based on solving business applications.

In the business-to-business arena, business is conducted between organizations or institutions only in a formal, transactional sense. Individuals, and sometimes groups of individuals, make the actual decisions. And individuals are looking for long-term relationships based on an understanding of their business problems. Mass marketing approaches are simply not productive in this environment.

The third trend, the growing importance of integrated marketing programs, arises from the emphasis on improved productivity that has characterized the '90s. Programs integrating all marketing and communication tools benefit both the buyer and seller. The buyer benefits by getting exactly the level and type of communication, information, and service that fit his or her needs and business applications. The seller benefits since this helps build customer loyalty, creates a more interdependent relationship, reduces selling costs, and improves profitability.

The developments shaping these trends include:

1. A greater number of contacts needed to make a sale. Buyers are requiring more information and are taking longer to make decisions because product features often have less differentiation and business solutions are more complex. This naturally leads to longer-term relationships as opposed to one-time transactions, or events.

2. Sales training costs are increasing as products continue to become more complex.

3. Fewer qualified, effective salespeople are available, especially for high-technology products.

4. The emergence of lower-cost relational databases and lower-cost data storage make it more economical to focus on the individual.

5. More managers are demanding accountability from sales and marketing.

6. Increasingly sophisticated and easier-to-use databases make it practical to identify existing and emerging market niches with greater focus.

7. Product life cycles are shorter, with the result that time—to disseminate information—is at a premium. For example, in the personal computer laptop market, the product life cycle has dropped to about eight months.

8. Organizations have flattened and decentralized decision making.

CUSTOMER RETENTION AND RELATIONSHIPS: AN ECONOMIC REALITY

In today's competitive arena, you cannot afford to only operate as a product-focused company. Being competitive today requires a renewed focus on building long-term relationships with customers. The keys to business success today, and in the coming decade, are to build a loyal customer base, ensure that product or service offerings meet customer needs, have an ongoing competitive intelligence system, have effective and efficient sales/distribution channels, and build new business around current customers.

On the surface, this can be, and has been, characterized as becoming customer focused, which is one of the many buzzwords one hears used to describe this change. But it means much more. It means building an *interdependent relationship* with the customer in which each relies on the other for business solutions and successes. The customer values the relationship and believes in it. You create a common bond with the individual customer based on a shared "win-win" approach and the customer trusts you. This is building a *customer community*. This is building long-term strategic relationships.

Building long-term strategic relationships with the customer is the key to staying competitive. If you do not take this approach, you are putting your business at risk. It is not an option. If you don't, your competitors will. Following a path of emphasis on events and transactions rather than relationships will lead to a steady erosion of your customer base and higher sales costs to revenues. Adopting an attitude that no one else in your industry is currently doing this will put you on the outside looking in.

This concept of customer community is not some ethereal psychological abstraction or huggy-feely management fad. It is based on hard, economic reality. The company that retains more of its customers, and understands individual customer needs, wants, and purchasing behaviors, is going to prosper.

For example, studies done by Bain & Company,[2] management consultants, and Technical Assistance Research Programs (TARP), a Washington, D.C., consulting firm,[3] demonstrate that retaining customers produces increased profits. These studies show that retaining an additional 2 percent of customers has the same effect as cutting costs by 10 percent.[4]

Similarly, studies done by the Service Management Group at the Harvard Business School show that customer retention can lead to customer loyalty.[5] And loyal customers generate increased revenues and profits. They become the foundation of your business.

CHANGING HOW YOU DO BUSINESS

Along with this growing awareness of the value of customer retention, dramatic changes have taken place in the way in which companies do business. Companies, both large and small, are moving away from the familiar adversarial buyer-seller relationships toward ones that resemble partnerships.

Today, more buying decisions are being made on total product or business solution cost, rather than price. Buyers are interested in customer service and support issues and look for value in the relationship. And buyers are constantly redefining what that value is.

These changes in the way companies do business have even extended beyond the traditional buyer-supplier relationships to include competitors. For example, IBM sells its components to competitors, such as Hitachi, Apple, and Canon. Unisys buys mainframe chips from IBM to use in systems that compete with IBM's.[6] IBM and Apple joined forces on the development of the Power PC.[7]

How can a company become a part of this? How does one go about building a customer community? If you look at the shelves of any large bookstore, you will see a number of books on the many facets of relationship marketing. While all discuss the importance of relationships and change, none focus on the desired end-points and the processes or steps necessary to accomplish this. That's what this book provides; a blueprint of tasks, processes, tools, behaviors, and leadership actions needed to build a customer community.

THE NEW PARADIGM: $n = 1$

Building a strategic relationship with the customer starts with a simple premise: marketing to individuals rather than accounts; focusing on the process of marketing to individuals. This process-driven approach represents a major change in the way companies handle marketing.

All marketing is direct marketing, direct to the individual. This has a dramatic impact on a company's sales success. The reason is simple: it is through the individual that you get to the business application for your product or service. The value of any individual is directly tied to the business application he or she manages and it is the individual acting on the business applcation with your product that creates value for the customer. Therefore, you need to focus on these individuals and their business applications rather than on the company or account.

This approach emphasizes a market segment size of one; i.e., $n = 1$ or the individual. In other words, concentrating on the individual is the path to increased sales. Dick Alberding, who was in charge of worldwide sales and marketing at Hewlett-Packard in the mid- and late 1980s, said that it wasn't until Hewlett-Packard followed this approach and changed its focus to the individual that they began to experience real success with printer products. At the core of this customer focus, Hewlett-Packard brought the customer into the product design process through its Customer Information Center.

However, embracing this $n = 1$ marketing and sales concept means a fundamental shift in attitudes. It involves moving from a "get the order, no matter what it takes" culture to one that emphasizes providing the best solutions to the individual customer, even if the solutions are someone else's.

For some in business-to-business marketing this is a monumental change. They have measured and rewarded a "push the product through the channel" approach for so long that shifting to a "How can I help the customer?" mindset represents a cultural change that is difficult to put into place.

When faced with this change, companies question if they can make this kind of investment; i.e., "We just don't have the resources." The reality of the marketplace is that, today, businesses cannot afford anything less than an uncompromising focus on the customer. To do less puts your business at risk.

It is only when you can begin viewing the customer as an individual, and not as a market segment or account or sale, that you can begin to move toward building a customer community. Customer community is built one person at a time. It is not a mass effort, but an individual and personal effort, nurturing each customer along the path to community. It is a journey, or expedition, that is well planned and filled with new experiences. It has an ever-present focus on more closely bonding with the customer.

THE EVOLVING COMMUNITY CONCEPT

This focus on the individual naturally evolves into the concept of community, which is a relationship or group of relationships based on a common bond or shared values. In the customer community this means that you and the customer have a shared commitment to work together to help each other succeed. You become more encouraging and service-focused—a new balance based on the integrity of your relationship.

The Basics of Customer Community

Figure 1-1 depicts the customer community journey as a series of sequential actions, though in practice they do not necessarily follow the same sequence. Many steps can and often do occur simultaneously and at different levels and intensities.

Identifying your customer. The first step in this process is to identify who your customers are. Surprisingly, not many companies know who their customers are. For example, many companies sell through distributors or independent sales channels, who mistakenly believe they own the customer

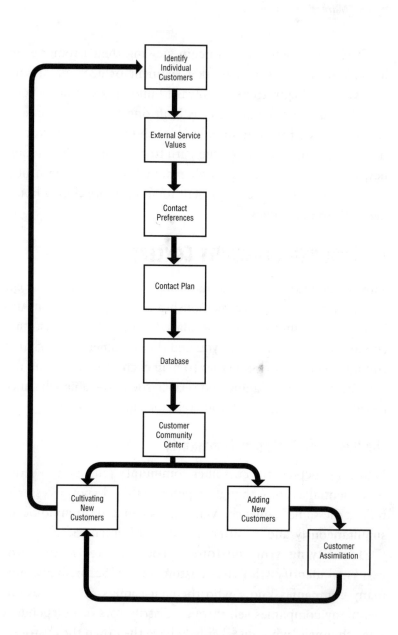

Figure 1-1 The Customer Community-Building Process

relationship and hide the customer from the manufacturer. Yet, it is the manufacturer that must continue to create value in their business. Also, the manufacturer's detachment from the customer, or end user, directly contributes to products being less adaptive to customer needs and weakens the value delivered by the manufacturer and reseller.

An important distinction needs to be made here: the customer is *not* the reseller. The customer is the individual who creates business value through the use of your product or service. This focus on the individual steward who is responsible for a business application is also helpful in understanding the economics of marketing and sales.

Another consideration is that not every name on your customer list is a customer. Rather, you need to distinguish between those who made a purchase years ago and those who are *active* customers. A number of measurements can be used to define a customer, but two must always be used: time and dollars. (For example, an active customer might be one who spent $100 in the past three months.) The most dependable measurements are recency of purchase, frequency of purchasing, and economic value of purchases or products purchased (e.g., two $100 purchases of products X and Y within the past six months).

Next, you need to recognize that it is not an account or organization but an individual who is the buyer, influencer, decision maker, specifier, etc., of your product/service. Once you make this shift in perspective, you can appreciate the subtleties that affect the buyer-seller relationship. As part of this process, organize your customer list by individual names within buyer groups/business applications, then within locations, and *finally* by accounts or companies.

Determining external service values. External service values represent those aspects of your product or service that drive purchasing behavior. These are the underlying reasons why a customer buys from you and not from someone else. To identify external service values, first understand your customer's needs. You need to know what their basic needs are and what needs you satisfy that the competition does not or cannot satisfy.

Determining external service values provides you with a powerful marketing tool. First, once you know what the customer values about your relationship, you can use that information to ensure that you deliver information and contacts that meet the customer's specific needs. It puts you in a better position to effectively tailor your message to address that customer's specific set of needs.

Another dimension of this approach is that it changes the way in which customers are segmented. Rather than simply using quantifiable segmentation criteria, such as SIC codes, employee size, sales volume, and so on, you can use qualitative criteria based on buying behaviors and common sets of customer needs, which are the needs satisfied by the external service values. Basing segmentation on these criteria has worked because it creates a coarse grouping of customers with similar communication and servicing requirements. Focusing on the individual creates this more granular segmentation into separate neighborhoods in the customer community grouped around common needs and purchasing behaviors.

Identifying customer contact preferences. One mistaken assumption illustrated in the United Airlines commercial is its emphasis on face-to-face contact. As the commercial points out, insensitivity to customers can spell disaster. However, face-to-face contact is not necessarily the right solution. As will be shown in depth later in this book, customers first want *quality contact,* i.e., value-based communication. For some types of contacts, that may mean face-to-face, but for other contacts, phone, fax, mail, or e-mail may be preferable. So, it's important to understand how your customer wants to be contacted.

Developing a value-added contact plan. Once you understand why and how an individual customer buys from you, you can begin the process of delivering value through every contact with the individual. This added value encompasses communicating with the individual and satisfying needs.

During this process, you need to identify every point of contact you have with the customer. Then you can analyze the type of information or value exchanged at each contact point. Next, ask the customer how, when, and about what they want contact to build and sustain a long-term relationship. You can then develop a detailed contact plan built around the customer's preferences.

Contacts are information pathways. *Whoever owns these vital pathways owns the relationship with the customer.* Adding value at every point of contact begins to build an interdependence between you and the customer. The customer begins to realize that they are receiving something in return every time they have contact with you. This translates into positive feelings. Just as in any interpersonal relationship, when you have positive feelings about another person who shares a set of values with you, you are attracted to that person. From the customer's perspective, he or she may become dependent upon you to provide solutions to their business problems. Your customer will become dependent upon you for information and wisdom. By assuring that each contact delivers value, the customer is encouraged to have contact with you.

On the other hand, if you mail or contact your customer and do not deliver value, you begin to *vaccinate* them against you and your future mailings, phone contacts, and visits. You behaviorally condition them to not value your relationship. Once immunized, their "thick skin" fails to react to future messages and they become an expensive sales challenge.

Creating value in the relationship. When you use the customer community approach, the customer knows that every contact through phone, fax, mail, or face-to-face meeting is worth it to them. And, when you have a face-to-face meeting with the customer, it is leveraged by value-based information that has been acquired in every contact you have had with them. They know your sales representative will be prepared to discuss specific issues of concern to them. This becomes a civil and productive way of doing business.

Designing a database. The customer database, where customer information is stored, is indispensable for building a customer community. A good database is a literal treasure chest of customer-specific information, including a complete history of each customer order, demographics, and detailed information collected during contacts with the customer. By capturing this type of information, when you have a contact with the customer you can use the database to deliver value to the customer.

An essential aspect of the database is its use. Too often, companies become highly protective of their customer database and limit access to it. In the customer community, the database must be open to and used by basically everyone in the organization—everyone who has direct contact with the customer.

From the customer database, you can extract information critical for new product development, target market segmentation, communication program development, new business acquisition, existing customer cultivation, and a myriad of other marketing and sales functions. It makes you more responsive to customer inquiries because the customer, buyer group, and account information are easily and quickly accessible.

Creating a customer community center (C³). At the center of this process is the Customer Community Center (C³). It is here that all marketing and sales activities are coordinated and implemented. The center is used to coordinate contacts with the customer, initiate "dialogue," respond to customer requests, execute direct mail and other marketing communication activities, schedule sales calls, perform direct selling functions, and monitor customers' changing needs or dissatisfactions.

One goal of the center is to increase sales productivity, which is measured by comparing sales expenses with sales revenues. Companies can experience an immediate 15 percent increase in sales productivity when they integrate phone and mail contacts with face-to-face contacts. Replacing some face-to-face contacts with four to six times as many phone and mail value-based contacts drives down sales expense, increases the frequency of customer contact, and raises perceived service levels.

A second goal is to increase the perceived value, satisfaction, and loyalty of your customers. Increased frequency of *value-based* contacts helps build a stronger customer relationship. Thus, the C^3 delivers increased sales productivity and improved customer loyalty at the same time.

For the C^3 to be effective, a community spirit must be a part of the culture. The people who staff and support the center must care about the customer, understand the customer's needs, know how to deliver value, and have a behavioral profile to act on that knowledge to delight the customer. In a C^3 with a community spirit, you will see an eagerness to listen to the customer, to set one's own agenda, and to truly serve the customer. It's a personal attitude and organizational and leadership style. The customer senses the difference. Integrity, encouragement, and trustworthiness are the *soft* measures.

Cultivating existing customers. An indisputable fact of business-to-business marketing is that your best source for new business is your current customer. The cultivation process takes advantage of this by actively searching out sales opportunities through existing, satisfied customers and by closely monitoring the relationship.

Your relationship with existing customers can be expanded through two strategies—penetration and retention. First is product and account penetration. Product penetration involves discussing with the customer other related products or services you offer that fit the customer's needs. This focus on customer needs serves to move the process from self-serving selling to customer-serving solutions.

The same principle is true for account penetration. It involves the customer identifying other individuals within their organization who may have a need for your products or services. When you have successfully cultivated the relationship with your customer and have built a spirit of community, your customer will choose to become an "apostle," referring potential customers both within and outside of the organization.

The second strategy is retention. Retain your best customers. Find out why some customers defect and why others stay with you. Identify which are the best customers to save and learn how to save them. Knowing how to keep your best customers is the key to a successful retention program.

Acquisition: Adding new members to the community. Efficiently acquiring new customers that fit into your customer community is only possible through knowledge of, and retention of, current customers. New or prospective customers should look like your best current customers.

The first step in the acquisition process is identifying valued customer attributes. In other words, develop a profile of your best customers and then look to match that. In short, this profile enables you to know where to look first.

This process includes examining your competitive position, creating an offer based on current customer external values, and then creating a contact plan to penetrate the target market segment. The contact plan leads to media selection since it is built on a process that defines what media are the most economically effective to use.

It is most effective to use the full range of media from publicity to advertising to direct mail to telemarketing in an integrated, continuous approach to acquisition. That is, don't rely on a single communication medium to generate leads, but rather use a full complement of tools that target messages to meet the perceived needs of each potential customer segment and, ultimately, each customer.

After initial contact, the C^3 is used to qualify leads and advance the selling process. The center also monitors and measures lead generation to track media effectiveness and provide sales channel accountability.

The final stage of the acquisition process is assimilation. Once a prospect has purchased from you, the customer is brought into the customer community. This initial "bonding" with the customer produces valuable shared information. From that point, you move into cultivation, during which you and the customer get to know each other better and hopefully find a broad long-term business foundation.

USING THE C^3 IN AN INTEGRATED PROGRAM

The Customer Community Center is the key to achieving the ends of customer retention and loyalty. It is an example of form following function. You cannot put a C^3 in place and then figure out how to use it. Rather, you first have to understand your customers' needs and your service and market applications. Job definitions, reward structures, and behavioral types for staffing then follow. Finally, you determine the best structure and size of the C^3 to meet your objectives.

Figure 1-2 is the model of a Customer Community Center. It integrates all the functions involved with the process of customer contact. The center of the C^3 is the database, where all information collected from the customer is stored. The central functional group, classified as operations, typically includes the telemarketing and account management functions. This is then supported by the other functional groups, including communciations management, printed response, technical support,

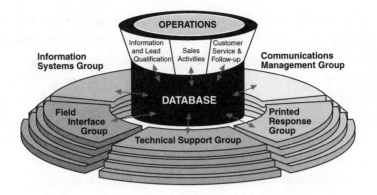

Figure I-2 Customer Community Center Model

© Hunter Business Direct, Inc.

field interface, and information systems. All functional groups have access to all information in the database.

The Database

The C³'s database is built upon individual customers and must be supported at four levels:

- The individual level, where a record of all contacts with the individual is maintained.

- The buyer group level, which is typically the individual's functional role and is where the business need or application resides, is the economic focus.

- The location level, which is the physical address of where the individual is located.

- The account level, which is the organization that the individual works within.

The database is more than just a place to capture customer information. It is the prime driver in account management, driving the quantity and quality of all customer contacts including mailings, faxes, and both phone and field contacts with customers and prospects. All transaction information is maintained at the individual level. Attribute information, such as SIC category and number of employees, can be included at any level of the database.

The database is nurtured by three primary types of contact—information and lead qualification, sales activities, and customer service and follow-up:

- Information and lead qualification. Information is obtained through any of the media channels including inbound or outbound telemarketing, trade shows, advertising, etc. All contacts with the individual are recorded in the database.

- Sales activities. All sales-related contacts including account management, telesales, and order taking are added to the database.

- Customer service and follow-up. This covers all problems the individual has with the selling organization whether related to billing, shipping, accounting, or other value-based contacts. Complaint handling and problem resolution are a major part of this.

Functional Interfaces

The C^3 takes those functions that have to be present in order to implement a marketing and sales system and integrates them, instead of having them operate as fragmented departments. Each function has an owner within the C³.

Companies that set up and operate a C³ can initially expect 40 percent of inbound calls to be order-specific, i.e., customers calling about ship dates, order status, billing, etc. Another 40 percent of inbound calls will be product- or application-specific: that is, customers calling for literature, additional product specs, pricing, and application support. A high number of calls are repetitive and, once they are documented, can often be handled on the spot by frontline telemarketing representatives.

This distribution seems to be true in almost any type of industry. What this means when setting up a C³ is that you may not need people with technical backgrounds for all the positions. In fact, only about 8 percent of the product-specific incoming calls usually require a degreed technician.

The five functional areas supported by the C³ include:

1. *Communications management group:* develops direct marketing programs for the company. Takes input from business units or product managers on types of marketing programs needed. Coordinates the implementation of the programs. Activities can include determining customer selects to use from the database, developing lead generation programs, designing standard personalized letters, designing and developing literature, defining telemarketing guides, designing and analyzing measurements, and providing program training and instructions.

2. *Printed response group:* performs all mail room functions for printed material. Stocks, mails, and reorders literature, tapes, disks, CDs, and other support material. Personalized letters "package" the response material.

3. *Technical support group:* answers technically specific questions from customers, users, and channel members who may have need for more specific or detailed technical support. May have specific customer assignments, i.e., be assigned to specific key accounts where inbound calls are automatically directed to a specific technical service person. Questions and answers are maintained in the C^3 database for access by the frontline phone support.

4. *Field interface group:* provides a central personal contact for sales reps, dealers, jobbers, franchises, national accounts, wholesalers, and retailers to interface with the C^3. It supports sales management functions to coordinate account planning activities between the customer and field salesperson.

5. *Information systems group:* interfaces with communications networks and the order management database. Maintains the internal network linking the functional groups with the database. Provides software support including compiling a combined marketing database for all business units, providing related accounting functions, tracking products and programs/inventory, reporting results, gathering sales and customer information from all functional groups, and providing multiple selects of stored data.

The underlying purpose of the Customer Community Center is to make it easier for the customer to do business with you. But it is much more than just hardware and software. It is people who use all the tools of the C^3 for building trust, loyalty, and a sense of community in their customer relationships.

COMMUNITY FROM THE INSIDE OUT

Building and sustaining a sense of community with customers depends on an internal community. If the people who contact the customer do not have a community mindset, they will not be able to build a spirit of community with customers.

The critical element is a customer focus, which must permeate the organization and become a part of its culture. Every person from the president to the lowest-paid shipping clerk within the organization must be committed to delivering value and customer satisfaction.

The sense of community must start at the top. If management's attitude is "How can we take advantage of employees?" then community will fail. Rather, management's attitude must be one of a cooperative partnership with employees and its role must be one of servant-leadership.

One can see key indicators of an organization's commitment to building community with its customers. First, internal groups are matched with customer groups. For example, Dell Computer has different groups serving customer groups, such as government, health care, manufacturing, retail, and so on.

Similarly, Toshiba America Information Systems, Inc., has separate product offerings, packaging, literature, channel support systems, and service groups for commercial and retail customers who have different needs for laptop computers. Each group deals with meeting the needs of specific customer groups.

These groups, or neighborhoods, are able to form strong bonds with the customer since they are dedicated to learning more about the customer's business. These groups also focus on building long-term relationships with the customer. It's reflected in all sorts of ways:

- Separate industry-specific marketing groups that become intimately familiar with their customer needs.

- When a customer's file appears on a computer screen, it shows behavioral (i.e., qualitative) information not typically recorded in customer files, such as a customer's needs and the purchasing behavior of the buyer group.

- Internal group discussions focused on individuals within customer organizations, not just attributes of the account organization. Once again, it's an individual focus.

- Phone contact representatives make suggestions to product marketing on product development to fulfill customer's existing or even emerging needs.

In a community environment, these groups interact with other members of the organization, such as research and development, manufacturing, shipping, quality control, accounting, etc., on a regular basis. They share customer satisfaction survey data with others in the organization as part of the process of continuous improvement. These groups focus on retaining, celebrating, and growing existing customers.

These people have a sense of being important parts of the organization. They believe that what they are doing is important. They have a vision, they talk with authority, and they take pride in their work. Their focus is not on a new customer, but on customer loyalty. They are measured and recognized for this focus. They are rewarded for customer behavior and results that create corporate profit and growth. Think about what a novel idea this is.

A Customer's View of Community

The community view from a customer's perspective is quite different from the typical buyer-seller relationship. First, the customer trusts the supplier to have his or her best interests at heart and not the supplier's own self-serving interests. This trust leads the customer to consider the supplier an extension of their organization, a part of the customer's community.

The adversarial buyer-seller relationship is gone. Rather, you work in a partnership, each contributing to the success of that partnership to bring value to the customer. For example, the customer invites this type of supplier to sit in on product planning sessions for their ideas in the product development process.

An example of this is Team TBA, which was set up as a new company to market tires, batteries, and accessories for Shell Oil. First they invited all the vendors to meet with them. They made it clear they were not expecting any proposals. Rather, they wanted to discuss this new relationship.

Two days were set aside to meet with the vendors. The first day, Team TBA met individually with each vendor to find out more about them. That evening a dinner was held for all vendors. In some cases, it was the first time that competitors had personally met.

The next day, each vendor learned how Team TBA wanted to conduct business. For example, one specification was that an electronic data interface (EDI) would be necessary as all transactions would be electronic. Vendors also learned they would be accountable for shipping deadlines and other aspects of order fulfillment. Other topics covered included forecasting and credit requirements, damaged goods procedures, and product line offerings. Finally, performance requirements were defined for the relationship and an agreement was sought on how each party's performance would be measured.

When this process was finished, each vendor was asked to review these requirements and submit a proposal within 30 days. The net result is Team TBA built a community with its vendors. Everyone knows what to expect in the relationship and how each will be judged.

Another aspect of community is that the customer responds to you in personal ways. For example, it is not uncommon for a customer to chide a telemarketing representative for being a little late on a regularly planned phone call. The customer has come to expect that they will receive a call at a certain time each week, and actually looks forward to it. Birthday cards, photos, and thank-yous are often exchanged.

THE NEW MARKETING VISION

Community is a new marketing concept that delivers impressive benefits as a result of integrated one-to-one marketing, contact databases, and value-based marketing. This approach enables you to build strategic relationships with the customer. When you develop a strategic relationship, you create barriers to entry that are difficult to scale. In fact, these become like buttes. You will work with your customer on a plateau with a steep, vertical climb for anyone wanting to reach your level.

This challenging goal does not rely on events or activities. It is a new state of mind that marketers must embrace. You won't achieve this by hiring a new customer service manager, going to a customer loyalty seminar, or by designing a new customer satisfaction survey. To get to community, you have to rethink and rebuild the fundamental aspects of your business from the inside out.

Two models, the Service-Profit Chain (Figure 1-3) and the Integrated Marketing Process (Figure 1-4), illustrate the central ideas and processes of the Customer Community and provide the framework for implementing it. Each, outlined here, is discussed more fully in the rest of this book.

The Service-Profit Chain, developed by the Service Management Interest Group at Harvard Business School, shows the interrelationship of a company's two communities, internal and external. To start, you look at the desired outcomes—revenue growth and profitability. Customer loyalty produces these outcomes. And that is the key emphasis of this model: how to achieve customer loyalty that translates into revenue growth and profits.

It shows that customer satisfaction is the key driver of loyalty, and that is only possible when you have provided the customer's external service values. External service values are a core issue as they identify why the customer buys from you.

Delivering external service values is dependent upon a company's internal operating strategy and service delivery system. In short, your employees are key to providing external service values. Both employee productivity and employee retention are key factors. For example, studies show a direct correlation between customer retention and employee retention.

And you need satisfied employees to achieve retention and productivity. Employee satisfaction relies on focused delivery of internal service values, which are the tools and environment that enable employees to do their jobs, i.e., productively delivering value to the customer. This is where management, or leadership, enters the picture. The leadership must be supportive of the internal service values and the employees.

The Service-Profit Chain offers convincing evidence that customer satisfaction and customer loyalty are the key ingredients for business growth and success. These ideas are explored more fully in Chapter 2.

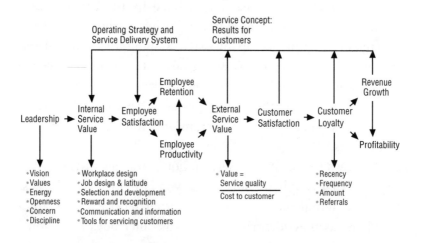

Figure 1-3 Service-Profit Chain

Source: Adapted and reprinted by permission of *Harvard Business Review*. An exhibit from "Putting the Service-Profit Chain to Work," by James L. Heskett, Thomas O. Jones, Gary Loveman, W. Earl Sasser, Jr., and Leonard A. Schlesinger, March–April 1994, p.166 © copyright 1994 by the president and fellows of Harvard College. All rights reserved.

The other model, the Integrated Marketing Process, shows the steps necessary to create a customer community. It closely parallels the concepts in the Service-Profit Chain.

This model has two tracks: one for customer retention and the other for acquisition. The steps for customer retention are covered in Chapters 3 through 7. Chapter 8 discusses acquisition.

In the retention part of the model, you start with understanding your market and then develop marketing plans. Note that the database is at the center of the model, both receiving and generating information. One of the first steps in retention is to segment and economically grade your customers. This enables you to better control how much is spent to support each customer.

Understanding needs and contact preferences is another step, similar to identifying external service values in the Service-Profit Chain. Once you have identified the customer's contact preferences, you need to balance that with the customer's economic value. It is through this process that you develop a mixture of contact tools—mail, fax, telephone, and face-to-face.

The next steps are the operational ones and include developing an integrated program of value-based contacts, implementing the plan, strengthening your relationships/bonds with the customer through the plan, and, finally, measuring and evaluating the results.

In the planning stages for acquisition, the key is to develop a profile of your target prospect by using your database of existing customers. You want to attract prospects that most closely resemble your best customers. It is through this that you can identify target segments and segment needs. Then, you need to reconcile the needs/benefits and the reason to act with the target segment.

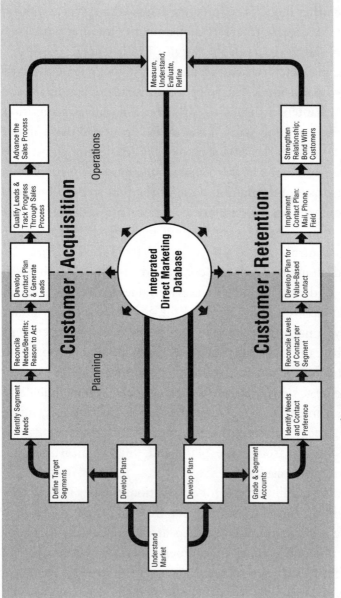

Figure 1-4 Integrated Marketing Process Model

© Hunter Business Direct, Inc. Developed by J. M. McIntyre.

In the operational stage, you develop a contact plan to generate leads, qualify and track leads, and advance the sales process that turns leads into buyers. Again, measurement and evaluation is a critical part of the process.

In both retention and acquisition, you have to remember that you are dealing with individual buyers, not accounts. Segmentation and targeting are predicated on an understanding of the individual. It is acting at the individual level that leads to developing the customer community.

Compelling economic reasons propel this journey to community. By building strategic relationships, you retain your best customers and build customer loyalty, which increases revenues and profits. You also create a bond with the customer that is difficult and expensive for competitors to fracture through special discounts and other price-driven selling and marketing tactics.

Ask yourself these questions: Have you written down who is a customer? Have you segmented markets on customer needs and behavior? Do you know why customers in each segment buy from you? Do you know the economic value of each customer? Do you have an integrated, value-based contact plan for each customer grade?

Next ask yourself: How healthy is your business? What percent of your customers defect each year? What penetration of product and buyers do you have in each customer account? How many referrals did you get last quarter?

Now, ask yourself: How sustainable is your business? In a time of rapid-fire downsizings, mergers, acquisitions, and divestitures, it is a natural question to ask. The answer is, in one sense, painfully simple: Customer relationships will define how sustainable your, or any, business is. The challenge is to act on the vision, to weave the programs you already have running into a new fabric. Acting may require a change in culture. Creating a community of customers—building business relationships based on a shared interdependence—is critical to sustained growth and profits.

Notes

1. "Kotler Foresees Integrated Future," *Business Marketing*, September 1993, 85.

2. Patricia Sellers, "Keeping the Buyers You Already Have," *Fortune*, Autumn/Winter 1993, 56–58.

3. John Goodman, Scott M. Broetzmann, and Dianne S. Ward, "Preventing TQM Problems: Measured Steps Toward Customer-Driven Quality Improvement," *National Productivity Review*, Autumn 1993, 555–571.

4. William H. Davidow and Michael S. Malone, *The Virtual Corporation: Structuring and Revitalizing the Corporation for the 21st Century* (New York: HarperCollins, 1992), 153.

5. James L. Heskett, Thomas O. Jones, Gary W. Loveman, W. Earl Sasser, Jr., and Leonard Schlesinger, "Putting the Service-Profit Chain to Work," *Harvard Business Review*, March–April 1994, 164–174.

6. Ira Sager, "IBM Knows What to Do with a Good Idea: Sell It," *Business Week*, 19 September 1994, 72.

7. Robert J. Berling, "The Emerging Approach to Business Strategy: Building a Relationship Advantage," *Business Horizons*, July–August 1993, 16.

2

THE ECONOMICS OF COMMUNITY

The driver for changing one's attitude and business practice to a focus on strategic relationships isn't just profits. It's survival. Building long-term strategic relationships with your customers is an economic necessity today. The strongest relationships are built on healthy interdependence. You don't have a choice— find your customers and build a business covenant.

In today's business world, with companies trying to rein in costs throughout their operations, many find marketing and sales costs still on the rise. This sets executives scrambling for answers. They start looking for more cost-cutting alternatives to the rising costs of advertising, direct mail, telemarketing, and, especially, the escalating costs of field sales. However, rather than randomly cutting costs, managers need to understand the underlying economic forces that drive up these costs and then structure marketing and sales processes to achieve cost efficiency while increasing effectiveness. The economic foundation for developing and managing the new way of doing business is to understand and act on creating value for your customers.

UNDERSTANDING THE COST OF SALES

The first step is to understand the cost of sales, which has been one of the most talked-about issues in business for years. It is also one of the most misunderstood aspects of marketing and sales. Most companies treat cost of sales simply as a percentage of total sales. Yet, it may cost that company up to 20 times more to sell a new customer than an existing customer. Companies typically do not make this distinction, rather they lump all sales costs into one category. This is a fatal planning and measuring error.

Another misunderstanding is management doesn't view marketing or sales the way it views other functions—as processes. Too often, companies approach marketing and sales with an event or transaction orientation. They focus on the sale, not the process. When companies begin to view marketing and sales as a process encompassing all aspects of customer contact—in both quantitative and qualitative terms—they can then plan, test, and measure results with the goal of continuous improvement. This process approach also makes for better forecasting.

The fact that sales costs are rising is indisputable. A number of studies, while estimating different absolute values for a sales call, show this continuing increase in the cost of a

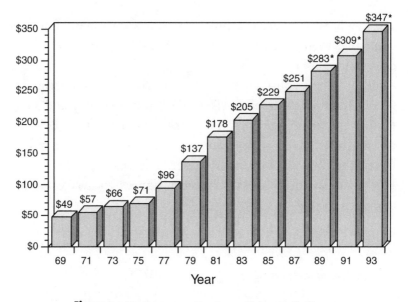

Figure 2-1 Business-to-Business Sales Call Costs

Source: Adapted from McGraw-Hill Research data.
*Estimates from industry experience.

face-to-face sales call. Probably the most familiar and most quoted sales call cost figures were provided by McGraw-Hill, which tracked business-to-business sales call costs for a number of years. Their data showed a continuing escalation of face-to-face sales contact costs (Figure 2-1).

Other cost-per-call studies show differing amounts. For example, in a study by Philip Kotler, he reported a high-tech company he worked with discovered it cost them $120,000 to support a salesperson. This included salary, commission, expenses, and fringe benefits. Based on this, they determined the company spent approximately $600 per sales call on a prospect. They also determined it took an average of three sales calls to convert the prospect into a customer. For this company, then, it costs more than $1,800 to acquire a new customer.[1]

Even when you factor in inflation, the cost of a business-to-business sales call has risen. As Rudy Oetting and Geri Gantman, principals of New York–based Oetting & Co., pointed out, since it takes more sales calls to close a sale today, the total selling cost is higher. They used the McGraw-Hill business-to-business sales cost figures to arrive at this comparison (Figure 2-2).[2]

	1979	1987
Cost of an industrial sales call	$137	$250
Factored for inflation (1987 $)	$235	$250
Number of appointments to a close	x4.3	x6.3
Cost per sale	$1,011	$1,575

Figure 2-2 Cost-Per-Call Inflation Comparison

Source: Adapted from Rudy Oetting and Geri Gantman, "Dial 'M' for Maximize," *Sales & Marketing Management,* June 1991, 106.

RECOGNIZING LIFETIME VALUE

While the rising costs of face-to-face sales calls are of concern, a greater concern should be how companies evaluate or value their customers. Rather than concentrating on quarterly sales figures, companies need to see customers in light of their *lifetime value.*

The concept of lifetime value (LTV) has been around for some time, primarily as a direct marketing tool, but in business-to-business marketing, it has only been in recent years that it has been treated seriously. Simply stated, LTV is the dollar value of a customer's purchases over the entire life of that customer's business relationship minus the acquisition cost and the cost to service that customer.

To illustrate this, assume the average life of a customer is five years. If that customer purchases $2,000 per year, and it cost $800 to acquire the customer with a yearly service cost (including product cost) of $1,600 (or 80%), then that customer's lifetime value is $1,200. (Note: to keep this example simple, present value of money is ignored.) So, if you retain that customer for five years, your income stream will be $1,200. If you don't retain the customer beyond the first year, your income stream is negative, with a loss of $400 (Figure 2-3).

The lifetime value of a customer is one of the major differences between consumer and business-to-business marketing. The lifetime value of a business-to-business customer normally far exceeds that of a consumer. Depending upon the product or service involved, a business-to-business customer may generate 20 times to several thousand times more revenue as a business buyer than as a consumer of a personal product or service.

During the 1970s and early 1980s, companies used LTV to manage acquisition costs and acquire more customers. In other words, LTV was viewed as dependent upon how much was spent on acquisition. The revenue stream for a newly acquired customer was *assumed*. For example, using the earlier example, if the cost of acquiring the customer could be

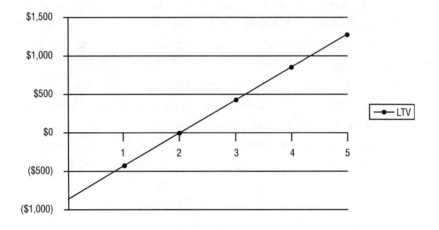

Figure 2-3 Cumulative Lifetime Value

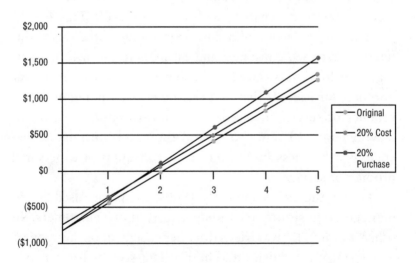

Figure 2-4 LTV Comparison

Original/Constant

	Year 1	Year 2	Year 3	Year 4	Year 5
Purchases	$2,000	$2,000	$2,000	$2,000	$2,000
Product Cost	1,600	1,600	1,600	1,600	1,600
Acquisition Cost	800	0	0	0	0
Net	($ 400)	$ 400	$ 400	$ 400	$ 400
LTV	−$ 400	0	$400	$800	$1,200

20 Percent Lower Acquisition Cost

	Year 1	Year 2	Year 3	Year 4	Year 5
Purchases	$2,000	$2,000	$2,000	$2,000	$2,000
Product Cost	1,600	1,600	1,600	1,600	1,600
Acquisition Cost	640	0	0	0	0
Net	($ 240)	$ 400	$ 400	$ 400	$ 400
LTV	−$ 240	$ 160	$ 560	$ 960	$1,360

20 Percent Increased Penetration First Year

	Year 1	Year 2	Year 3	Year 4	Year 5
Purchases	$2,000	$2,400	$2,400	$2,400	$2,400
Product Cost	1,600	1,920	1,920	1,920	1,920
Acquisition Cost	800	0	0	0	0
Net	($ 400)	$ 480	$ 480	$ 480	$ 480
LTV	−$ 400	$ 80	$ 560	$1,040	$1,520

reduced 20 percent, from $800 to $640, then the LTV of that customer would increase to $1,360, a 13 percent increase.

In a customer community, the focus shifts to increasing the LTV by increasing the amount the customer purchases. If, instead of lowered acquisition costs, the focus is toward increasing revenue by 20 percent, the result is dramatically different. Assume a 20 percent increase in annual revenue between the first year and the remaining years, i.e., rising from $2,000 to $2,400 in each of the remaining years. If product and service costs rise proportionally (80 percent), the annual contribution would be $480 ($2,400 minus 80 percent of $2,400). The result is LTV rises to $1,600, a 33 percent increase compared with a 13 percent increase with cutting costs. Figure 2-4 and the accompanying table summarize this comparison.

While acquisition costs are important, too often companies get caught up in the formulas and the model building. Today the foundation for profitability and sustainability is how to retain customers that have been acquired. In a customer community, the cost of servicing the customer (as a percentage of sales) actually goes down every year and the number of retained active customers increases within the account.

Of course, this is just a portion of the economic value of focusing on the customer. Longer active customer life, referrals, product penetration, and lower operating expenses contribute to additional increases in LTV.

One of the pitfalls associated with lifetime value is some base it on the premise that, once you acquire the customer, you own a revenue stream. This may be more true in consumer marketing, where a string of activities and events, such as mailings, offerings, etc., are paramount. But business-to-business marketing has more interrelatedness between the customer and the supplier. LTV is more dependent upon how the customer is treated, as that greatly influences how they choose to buy, what they choose to buy, and how long they choose to buy.

A further refinement that can be taken is determining the discounted lifetime value. By computing a *discounted* lifetime value (that is, the present value of expected income and expenses during the term of the relationship) of each customer, a company can understand more accurately what is happening to the size and value of its customer base.

LTV is a better indicator than sales statistics, which usually are a periodic revenue measure and indicate how customers have responded over a fixed time interval. Lifetime customer value, in contrast, is an asset measure. Determining the lifetime value of the customer base can help marketers judge their expenditures by measuring a plan's efficiency in producing assets.[3]

The sophisticated marketer will compute the lifetime value of each customer and then use that to measure growth each year against the standard model. By comparing the difference in the aggregate lifetime value of customers from year to year, companies have a better measure of performance than simply comparing gross sales revenues.

An example of this is the Shell Fleet Card. Shell was the first major oil company to introduce a vehicle fleet card for corporations. The card provided more detailed billing information for each corporate customer. For Shell, it provided the perfect database for calculating lifetime value, by tracking retention year-to-year and gallons of fuel purchased. However, if Shell had only looked at total cards in use, they could have missed even a double-digit percent defection in cardholders over a two-year period, which meant lost revenue and higher costs for acquiring new customers. With the database, Shell was able to use a customer retention program to reverse this.

To extend this example, a more accurate value for each corporate customer would have included their referrals and their value as an "apostle" in getting others to sign up for the card. Since customer acquisition is highly expensive in the card industry, tracking this "added value" of customers could have significant economic benefit.

THE ECONOMIC IMPACT OF RETENTION

The key to increasing lifetime value is customer retention and loyalty. Consider the studies done by Bain & Company, who have been in the forefront of research on customer retention and customer defection. Frederick Reichheld, who directs Bain's loyalty practice, stated: "Taking customer defections out of a business is like taking friction out of a mechanical system. Defections steal energy and dissipate performance. When you improve retention, you create a highly efficient machine."[4]

Customer retention is built on customer loyalty. A 5 percent increase in loyalty will change the profitability of a business by at least 25 percent. This means if you can move from having 60 percent of your customers active over a period of time to 65 percent active, you will experience significant increases in profitability.

A Bain & Company study looked at various industries and applied this 5 percent increase in retention. The results were lifetime profits would be nearly doubled in some industries with just a 5 percent increase in customer loyalty (see Figure 2-5).

As Reichheld noted: "Based on cash-flow analysis, you can measure the impact of improving customer retention in the same dollars-and-cents terms that you use to measure everything else."[5]

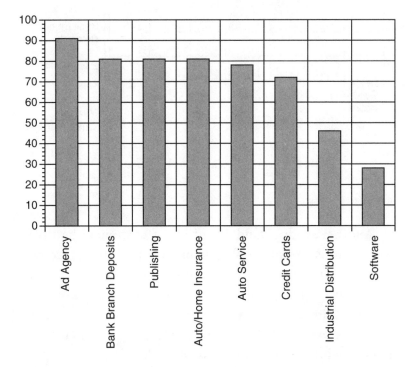

Figure 2-5 How Much a 5 Percent Increase in Loyalty Lifts Lifetime Profits per Customer

Source: Adapted from Patricia Sellers, "Keeping the Buyers You Already Have," *Fortune,* Autumn/Winter 1993, 58. Used with permission of Bain & Company, Inc.

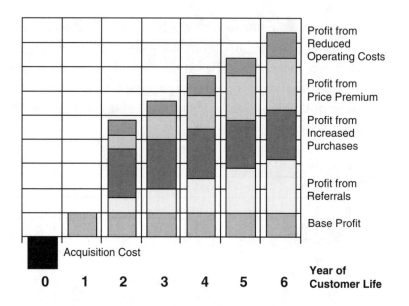

Figure 2-6 Profit Increase During Customer Life

Source: Bain & Company, Inc.

Another study found retention of customers had often been cited as the single biggest predictor of the future profitability of a company.[6] This can intuitively be seen because, as customer retention goes up, marketing costs go down. A company can concentrate fewer resources on acquiring new customers to replace the lost ones. Moreover, loyal customers frequently bring in new business.

The Bain & Company graphic in Figure 2-6 shows the reasons for this increased profitability through customer retention.

As can be seen in this example (and in Figures 2-3 and 2-4), during the first year of customer life, no profit is earned.

This is due to the acquisition cost for the new customer. Also, one experiences higher costs during the first year as the seller and buyer go through getting acquainted with one another. The next year sees only a basic profit return. It's not until the third year of the relationship that the customer becomes more than modestly profitable. It is here the relationship starts paying off in such areas as referrals, increased purchases, enhanced services, and lower operating costs. These only occur when one actively cultivates the customer relationship.

It is critical to this process to fully understand which customers are profitable and which are not. For example, a laboratory services company, after using an activity-based cost analysis, found their high-volume customers, who they thought were the core of their business, were, in fact, only marginally profitable. This was due in part to the intense competition in the commodity-type services segment. They also found they had a smaller, but growing, segment of customers who wanted higher margin, value-added services. This gave the company greater long-term profitability. As a result of this analysis, the company focused its resources and efforts on the value-added customers, which resulted in an increase in profits despite an initial decline in sales revenues.[7]

RETENTION AND ACQUISITION

When you focus on retention, you control lifetime value. When you focus on acquisition, you can end up in a death spiral. But, just focusing on customer retention and ignoring development and acquisition activities doesn't work either. You must have a balanced program that begins with customer retention, moves to customer cultivation, and then continues to build through acquisition. That's why the Customer Community Center is so important; profitable acquisition grows naturally out of an ongoing focus on your best customers.

With the knowledge of which customers are likely to be loyal also comes knowledge of which customers are not. Bain's Reichheld commented, "Companies can then direct resources away from customers who are not likely to stay."[8]

Using customer retention as a corporate strategy has an additional benefit. It, in effect, creates an exit barrier so that terminating the relationship becomes unattractive for the customer.

New business acquisition is so closely tied with customer retention that you can't have cost-effective acquisition until you first establish a retention program. Figure 2-7 summarizes the differences between a retention or cultivation approach and one focusing on acquisition.

As you move through the comparisons you can see the strategies for each are different. The first step in the process, and the most critical, is to define a customer. You need to know when someone becomes a customer and when they stop being an active customer. For example, a "customer" is *always* defined by dollars and/or product purchases within a given time frame, i.e., $1,000 within the past 12 months. Other criteria you can use might include "must make a second purchase within six months." You can then identify which of those customers you want to keep. Then you move to the process of cultivation, which enables you to expand your product line offerings to the individual customer, followed by expanding sales within the buyer's organization.

When you have an account cultivation process underway, only then should you look toward acquisition. For acquisition to be most successful, you have to know your best customers and then go after those potential customers who look the most like your best customers.

Retention	Acquisition
Nurturing relationships	Acquiring potential relationships
Internal research	External research
Demographic profiles + transaction history	Demographic profiles
Actual needs driven	Projected needs driven
Contacts must be personal	Contacts can be less personal
Accuracy required	Inaccuracy tolerated
Offer and relationship driven	Offer driven
Offers must be integrated	Offers can be events
Relatively high response rates	Relatively low response rates
Supports reactivation	Supports assimilation
Synergistic with acquisition	Synergistic with retention

Figure 2-7 Retention Strategy and Acquisition Strategy
© Hunter Business Direct, Inc.

Retention, and building loyalty, are keys to success for this new vision of business-to-business marketing. But, most important is to structure the business relationship on a sense of shared values that makes your competitors true "outsiders." Shared values are the passport to the customer community.

USING AN INTEGRATED APPROACH TO MINIMIZE SALES AND MARKETING COSTS

Building customer loyalty, increasing lifetime value, and driving down sales costs are then the three overriding goals for the customer community. The connection between loyalty and lifetime value is clear. However, the predicament is how to reduce sales costs as a percent of revenue without negatively impacting sales.

In building the customer community, an integrated marketing approach is used that capitalizes on the traditional marketing and sales tools. To reduce the overall cost of servicing or contacting the customer, a mix of the basic tools of fax, mail, and telephone leverages the higher-cost personal contacts. By reducing the number of face-to-face sales calls on a customer, while increasing the perceived service levels through supplementing face-to-face contact with more frequent mail and phone contacts, sales force productivity is increased. Companies with a field sales force can realize an immediate 15 percent decrease in sales expense to revenues through integrating their contacts in this manner.

Of course, a key factor is you don't want to diminish the customer's perception of service levels. In other words, you don't want the customer to think they are getting less attention. The reality is, with this approach, customers perceive they are getting more. The reason is simple; since it's less costly to make several phone contacts, you are significantly increasing the contact frequency while decreasing more costly face-to-face contacts.

One of the misconceptions people have about selling is the customer prefers face-to-face contact. This simply is not true. Arthur Andersen & Co. did a study on what elements of the buyer-seller relationship were important to the buyer. Over time, the importance of field sales contact changed (Figure 2-8). This does not mean field sales contact is any less important in the overall selling process, nor can it be replaced by telephone contacts. Rather, it means the customer prefers other contact media for certain *types* of information. Time has become more precious, so the new focus is on *access* and *responsiveness*.

Figure 2-8 also shows the role of the inside salesperson has grown significantly. This is an inevitable result of shifting nonselling tasks away from the sales force and using other forms of contact to deliver information.

Service	1970	1980	1985	1990
Contact with outside salesperson	First	Third	Fifth	Eighth
Frequency and speed of delivery	Second	First	First	Second
Price	Third	Second	Third	Fourth
Range of available products	Fourth	Fifth	Fourth	Third
Capable inside salesperson	Fifth	Fourth	Second	First

Figure 2-8 Contact Preferences

Source: Based on Arthur Andersen & Co. data.

This approach works in fast-growing industries, such as with Toshiba in laptop computers, as well as industries that some view as stagnant or dwindling, such as the typewriter market. For example, this was the situation facing Lexmark.

Lexmark, formed in 1991 through a leveraged buyout from IBM, is a $2 billion manufacturer of printers and related products. One of those products is typewriters. The typewriter group, which traces its roots to the revolutionary IBM Selectric typewriter, has more than 50 percent market share, but the market is dwindling. Yet, this is still a profitable business and it represents millions in revenues for Lexmark.

In July 1994, Lexmark launched an integrated marketing program to achieve three major goals. They wanted to reduce the sales expense-to-revenue ratio (or increase sales productivity), maintain or increase total revenue to plan, and increase customer (dealer) satisfaction.

Lexmark took several steps to pursue these goals. One was to analyze their current authorized dealers and categorize them by revenue potential. They decided to have their field sales representatives concentrate on the categories with the highest potential and use telemarketing and mail to support these dealers as well as categories with lower potential. In addition, telemarketing and mail would be used to support field sales. Lexmark developed a synchronized program integrating mail, phone, and field sales contacts to reach all dealers at least once per month with value-based contacts.

The results for the first 18 months of the program were encouraging. The sales expense-to-revenue ratio was reduced by 6.4 percent. Although short of their goal, it was a major step forward. Total revenues were 96 percent of the targeted goal, and were showing a growth trend in market share. And satisfaction, measured for dealers and for sales representatives, improved and surpassed the targeted goals. A revealing trend that emerged was inbound calls from dealers significantly exceeded expectations, despite not using an 800 number.

Although Lexmark has only had 18 months' experience with an integrated marketing program, the incremental gains they are seeing demonstrate the effectiveness of using an integrated program to increase sales productivity.

THE SERVICE-PROFIT CHAIN

Building customer loyalty while increasing sales productivity leads to increased profits. This is a simple economic fact. Achieving this outcome requires a systematic approach that redefines each element within marketing and sales. As mentioned earlier, marketing and sales must be considered a process. As with any business process, sustainable profits should be the end result. This is especially true of marketing and sales as they are the primary revenue generators for a company.

A model developed by the Service Management Interest Group at Harvard Business School shows how this process is built and how it achieves increased revenues and improved profits. While the model, the Service-Profit Chain (Figure 2-9), was developed mostly from consumer marketing data, our experience shows it applies very well to business-to-business marketing. In fact, this has proven to provide a structured way of explaining how to go about building sustainable strategic relationships with business-to-business customers.

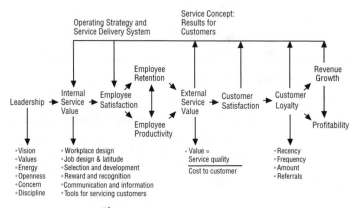

Figure 2-9 Service-Profit Chain

This is really a "map" for our journey that helps us understand the underlying principles of the Customer Community Center. Too often, people begin this process by moving left-to-right, i.e., starting with leadership and internal factors, then moving to revenue growth and profitability. The more successful route is to start with the desired outcomes of revenue growth and profitability, then move backward (right-to-left) through the process to determine how you can best achieve the results on the right. The following discussion takes this route.

CUSTOMER LOYALTY DRIVES REVENUE GROWTH AND PROFITABILITY

Not surprisingly, the first stage of the Service-Profit Chain recognizes that customer loyalty drives revenue growth and profitability. The Harvard research found three primary measurements of customer loyalty, which they refer to as the three "R's." Included are the stream of revenue and profits from retention of loyal customers, repeat sales, and referrals.[9] These closely parallel the four measurements that have been the cornerstones of business-to-business direct marketing for decades: recency of purchase, frequency of purchase, amount of purchase, and referrals. The tools, processes, and human competencies to build growing, profitable companies have been developed and refined by the master craftsmen of business direct marketing. They are your guides.

As has been previously explained, in building strategic relationships you need to take the relationship beyond the purchase. Most importantly, you must increase the breadth and depth of your relationship with the customer. For example, in the customer cultivation process, you first concentrate on increasing the number of buyers and the number of product lines sold at each location and then work on developing sales at multiple locations within the account.

Simply put, use existing customer relationships to generate new sales opportunities. This develops a closer relationship (loyalty) with the customer, which can be leveraged to gain lower-cost access to other buyers at the same location or account.

The second tactic is to listen to the customer and gain marketing knowledge from each contact with the customer. By paying attention to what the customer is saying, you can then develop new or improved product offerings to increase the breadth of products used at a single location. Listening enables you to better understand the customer's business application (buyer group) needs and problems.

A recent experience with Team TBA supports this. Team TBA markets non-petroleum products to Shell dealers. While the dealer principal may be the apparent customer, Team TBA focuses on the service bay mechanic as the strategy for increasing account penetration at each dealership. Building a relationship with the individual mechanic leads to referrals to other mechanics in the dealership, which expands the breadth of the relationship. They also focus on product penetration by making the mechanic aware of additional products sold through Team TBA. For example, while a mechanic may be using Shell-branded batteries, they may not be using Shell-branded oil filters or similar products. This expands the depth of the relationship.

Another important aspect of loyalty is determining which customers you want to keep. You need to be able to define the type of customer that has the potential of becoming a loyal customer. As Bain & Company's Reichheld noted, "Finding loyal customers requires taking a hard look at what kinds of customers a company can deliver superior value to. If the analysis is done well, that customer segment will be fairly homogeneous and that homogeneity improves the economics of serving the segment."[10]

CUSTOMER SATISFACTION DRIVES CUSTOMER LOYALTY

Customer loyalty is based on customer satisfaction. This may seem obvious, since a dissatisfied customer is not likely to become a loyal customer. But, bear in mind, not all satisfied customers will become loyal customers. Reichheld noted: "While it may seem intuitive that increasing customer satisfaction will increase retention and therefore profits, the facts are contrary. Between 65 and 85 percent of customers who defect say they were satisfied or very satisfied with their former supplier. . . . Current satisfaction measurement systems are simply not designed to provide insight into how many customers stay loyal to the company and for how long."[11]

How then does one measure customer satisfaction? First, this is not simply conducting a like/dislike or competitive ranking survey. Rather, you must focus on *behavioral measurements*. Measuring satisfaction based on the customer's purchasing behaviors and willingness to provide referrals is what provides meaningful information. This ties back into the four key customer loyalty measurements of recency, frequency, amount of purchase, and referrals.

Understanding Customer Satisfaction

While most executives and managers acknowledge the importance of customer satisfaction and the necessity to measure it, few understand the underlying principles of customer satisfaction as a marketing tool.

Customer satisfaction criteria can vary from industry to industry and from product type to product type. For example, Dataquest asked users in three product categories—semiconductors, PCs, and printers—to describe their most important concerns. In the semiconductor industry, high priority items for customers were reasonable prices, on-time delivery, quality, and a commitment from the vendor. For a PC customer, the emphasis was on value, quality, and a commitment from the vendor. Dataquest found technology issues, delivery, and documentation were judged less important. In printers, customers, while pleased with quality, were dissatisfied with value. They specifically mentioned the high cost of add-ons and options such as fonts, feeders, trays, and memory.[12]

Measuring Customer Satisfaction

Understanding customer expectations, and fulfilling them, are at the core of customer satisfaction. The Technical Assistance Research Project (TARP) has conducted numerous studies on customer satisfaction. One recent report discusses customer-driven quality, which it defines as: "the ability to consistently meet or exceed customer needs, wants, and expectations throughout the life cycle of the customer/company relationship, resulting in repurchase, brand loyalty, and positive word of mouth."[13]

The TARP report went on to state: "achieving customer satisfaction, continued customer loyalty, and long-term revenue streams depends on the consistent provision of products and services throughout the customer's relationship with the company—that is, product design, marketing, sales, delivery, customer service, billing, and many other areas all have a direct or indirect effect on quality, customer satisfaction, and continued customer loyalty."[14]

While customer satisfaction measurements give a company valuable information, they need to be approached with caution as they are often not true measurements of customer loyalty. Studies have shown little to no correlation exists between most customer satisfaction survey results and customer retention.

Two examples illustrate this lack of correlation. In the first, Toshiba dealers reported a high level of dissatisfaction with lack of product. Since product availability was an industry-wide problem and not one limited to Toshiba, dealers still displayed loyalty through the shortage and when product was again available.

In the other case, a company believed they were doing an excellent job of satisfying customers when, in reality, more than one-third of customers having problems were defecting. In this case, the company did a customer satisfaction survey measuring the customer's perception of service. However, they included a premium with the survey and sent it only to their best customers. Not surprisingly, they continually scored above 4.5 on a 5-point scale.

A better way to approach customer satisfaction is to ask questions you would ask when trying to assess if any of your customers are at risk. For example, instead of asking the customer if they are satisfied, ask them if they will buy from you again. This gives a better indicator of satisfaction. Next, ask them if they would refer you to other people. This type of question is more directly related to customer retention, which is based on behavior. People may lie to themselves about how they feel about a situation, but they are unlikely to lie to someone else.

When you take this approach, which differs from the traditional customer satisfaction like/dislike survey, you also have the opportunity to pinpoint areas of satisfaction. Part of this strategy is to conduct these types of surveys by phone, which enables the representative to ask key follow-up ques-

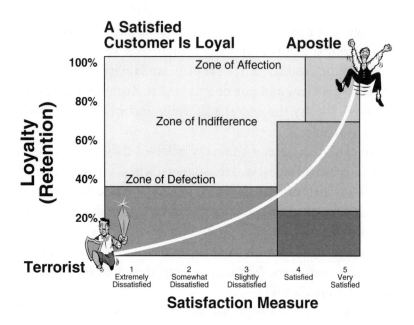

Figure 2-10 Loyalty/Satisfaction Chart

Source: Based on information from James L. Heskett. Adapted and used with permission of the Service Management Interest Group at Harvard University School of Business.

tions to uncover areas of dissatisfaction or areas of unmet expectations.

The limitations of the customer satisfaction measurement are documented by Heskett, et al., at Harvard. Using the standard 5-point rating scale, the Harvard researchers found when average scores were less than 4.5, customers were still at risk. Figure 2-10 shows this study.

In the chart, you can see that only when customers enter the "zone of affection" are they classified as loyal customers, and ultimately "apostles" for your company.[15]

EXTERNAL SERVICE VALUES DRIVE CUSTOMER SATISFACTION

External service values are those attributes of the relationship that drive a customer's purchasing behavior. In other words, these are the reasons customers buy from you and they, in turn, drive customer satisfaction.

In the customer community, the determination of external service values forms the foundation for doing business. Understanding what the customer values in the relationship not only encompasses those attributes attached to a product or service, but also involves how the customer is contacted. For example, knowing how the customer wants to be contacted, when, about what, and how often, enables you to add value to the relationship by meeting these customer preferences at the lowest cost.

Chapter 3 provides a more in-depth discussion of external service values.

EMPLOYEE PRODUCTIVITY AND LOYALTY DRIVE EXTERNAL SERVICE VALUES

Studies show a direct correlation exists between customer retention and employee retention. Bain & Company's Reichheld observed, "Customer retention and employee retention feed on one another."[16]

Harvard professor Leonard Schlesinger believes high turnover creates "a cycle of failure" because it results, at least temporarily, "in low productivity, low service, angry customers, and even more discontented workers."[17] His summary is seen in Figure 2-11.

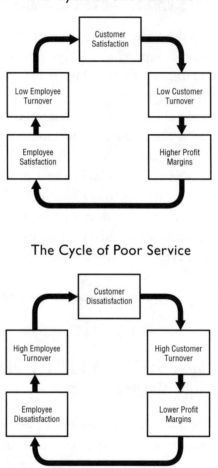

The Cycle of Good Service

Customer
Satisfaction

Low Employee
Turnover

Low Customer
Turnover

Employee
Satisfaction

Higher Profit
Margins

The Cycle of Poor Service

Customer
Dissatisfaction

High Employee
Turnover

High Customer
Turnover

Employee
Dissatisfaction

Lower Profit
Margins

Figure 2-11 The Cycles of Service

Source: Adapted from "Breaking the cycle of failure in services" by Leonard A. Schlesinger and James L. Heskett in *Sloan Management Review* 32:3, Spring 1991, pp. 18–19. Cited in Patricia Sellers, "What Customers Really Want," *Fortune,* 4 June 1990, 66–68. Used by permission of the publisher. Copyright 1997 by Sloan Management Review Association. All rights reserved.

EMPLOYEE SATISFACTION DRIVES EMPLOYEE LOYALTY AND PRODUCTIVITY

Researchers point out employee retention is the key to delivering customer satisfaction. And employee retention is based on employee satisfaction. The two critical elements of employee satisfaction are customer feedback and management support, or empowerment.

Customer feedback can be an incentive and motivator for employees and it contributes to employee satisfaction. It tells you how well you are doing. Customers relate to people and not to companies. They will respond to efforts on the part of an employee to be of help. In the case of the frontline employee, positive feedback from the customer will cause the employee to not only continue to take the action, but look for new ways to do it more efficiently.[18]

Employee empowerment, by itself, is a contributor to employee satisfaction. Knowing they have the authority to help customers solve problems gives employees satisfaction. However, this empowerment should not be given lightly. As one group of researchers noted, "The organization must train the people who interact with customers, and then it must empower them. That is, it must give them the authority, responsibility, and incentives to recognize, care about, and attend to customer needs."[19]

INTERNAL QUALITY DRIVES EMPLOYEE SATISFACTION

Employees are more loyal and productive when satisfied. However, achieving employee satisfaction entails an entire spectrum of considerations. These range from workplace design through rewards and recognition, all critical aspects of the Customer Community Center. Some of the more critical elements are:

- *Workplace design:* the key to workplace design is it should support delivery of value to the customer.

- *Selection and development:* studies show different behavioral types are needed for inbound and outbound telemarketing.

- *Reward and recognition:* providing appropriate rewards and recognition, based on customer results, is critical to employee satisfaction.

- *Tools:* includes the technology necessary to provide a convenient means of contact for the customer, the database for depositing customer information, and the equipment and means needed to maintain continuing contact with the customer.

LEADERSHIP SERVES THE PROCESS

The entire process outlined in the Service-Profit Chain Model relies on leadership. According to the researchers:

> Leaders naturally have individual traits and styles. But the CEOs of companies that are successfully using the service-profit chain possess all or most of a set of traits that separate them from their merely good competitors. Of course, different styles of leadership are appropriate for various stages in an organization's development. But the messages sent by the successful leaders we have observed stress the importance of

careful attention to the needs of customers and employees. These leaders create a culture capable of adapting to the needs of both."[20]

Unless its leaders drive the process, no company will be successful in customer service. To really deliver outstanding customer service means employees should not be focused on short-term profits. And, in order for employees to make that sort of paradigm shift, the leaders must provide continual demonstrations of support. As Davidow and Uttal note, "No company can produce outstanding service unless its top managers are visibly, constantly, and sometimes irrationally committed to the idea. Taking care of customers is so much work that it gets done only if the people at the top lead the charge."[21]

Leadership means truly serving the employee and the customer. Leadership must focus on getting frontline employees who work with the customer to own that relationship. The employee must be able to interpret needs and deliver solutions in an economically sustainable environment.

LINKING THE SERVICE-PROFIT CHAIN TO STRATEGIC RELATIONSHIPS

The Service-Profit Chain provides the conceptual model that underlies building a long-term strategic relationship. The Customer Community Center is the organizational unit that delivers this. It is the means through which a company can take full advantage of this model. It provides the organization with the ability to manage and coordinate all customer contacts.

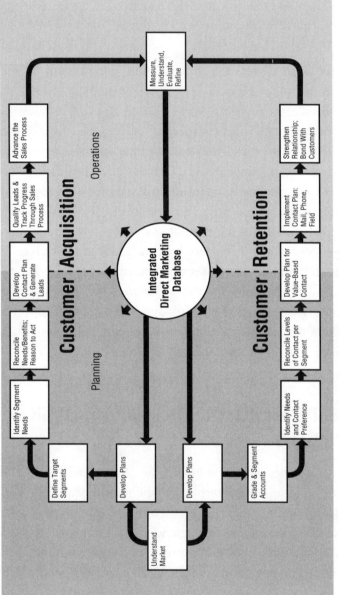

Figure 2-12 Integrated Marketing Model

© Hunter Business Direct, Inc. Developed by J. M. McIntyre.

A natural extension of the Service-Profit Chain is the Integrated Marketing Model (Figure 2-12), which shows the steps used in the process of building a customer community. These steps comprise the balance of this book.

The Integrated Marketing Model shows two primary paths—customer retention and customer acquisition. Keep in mind, a critical distinction exists between these. Most marketing people want to jump to the top of the model (the acquisition path) in the belief that getting customers is primary. Yet, in practice, the lower portion of the model—retaining existing customers—is the starting point.

In addition, the model shows planning steps (on the left side) and operational steps (on the right side). The planning steps basically involve acquiring customer information, interpreting it, and using it to design marketing programs. The operational steps implement the plans, initiate and maintain contact with the customer, and measure and evaluate the processes.

Customer Retention

Marketing database. At the center of both the retention and acquisition processes is the marketing database. Each step not only uses information from the database, but also contributes or adds to the database. The database is the central depository for *all* customer information. Chapter 5 shows how the database is constructed.

Understand the market. This goes beyond simply looking at markets from a broad perspective. It involves determining the specific reasons why customers purchase, what business application needs are satisfied through the purchase, and segmenting markets by clustering customers around common sets of needs. Chapter 3 discusses these topics.

Develop plans. Planning is the process of evaluating the environment, analyzing market opportunities, selecting target markets, developing marketing strategies, and planning marketing actions to implement the strategies. It has a direct link with the marketing database.

Segment and grade accounts. Within the customer community, the differences between customers must be considered. This involves segregating customers around common needs and purchasing behaviors as well as grading them into five categories based on value. Through this, active customers are identified and contact plans can be developed that take into account each customer's unique needs, behavior, and economic value. Chapter 4 has a detailed discussion of the process.

Identify needs/contact preferences. Understanding customers' needs and their contact preferences is critical to ensure value-based communication. This involves having customers identify their needs and how they want to receive infomation. Through this, value is added to the relationship. Chapters 3 and 4 cover these issues.

Reconcile contact levels per segment. Any marketing program must be economically justified. In this step, the customer's contact preferences are reconciled with expected customer revenues or value. This ensures contact media and frequency are economically justified. Chapter 4 shows how this is accomplished.

Develop plan for value-based contacts. A customer contact plan is developed that details the number and frequency of mail, phone, and face-to-face contacts each customer will receive, based on their economic value. Chapter 4 shows the model used for this planning.

Implement contact plan. The contact plan is implemented through the Customer Community Center using the appropriate mix of contact media, including mail, fax, phone, electronic mail, and face-to-face sales contacts. Chapter 6 describes how contact plans are executed.

Strengthen relationship/bond with customers. While the integrated marketing process contributes to building relationships through value-added contacts, strengthening that bond takes place during the "cultivation" process, during which customer-identified needs are used to expand the breadth and depth of product or service offerings. Chapter 7 outlines the steps in this process.

Measure and evaluate. A means to measure the effectiveness of programs and to continuously improve the process is essential for any business process. Different measurement tools are described throughout the book.

Customer Acquisition

Before moving on to customer acquisition, the customer retention program must be implemented. It is only then one can determine which customers are the most profitable and which product or service features deliver value to the customer and, in turn, drive purchasing behavior. When this knowledge is available, then the move to customer acquisition can be made since there is now a profile of which prospective customers to target. Rather than searching broadly defined market universes for potential prospects, this enables pinpointing target market segments and delivering a message that works. This is only possible because current customers have defined what is valuable in the relationship.

Through understanding and cultivating existing customers, you gain insight into your customer base or franchise. It is through this process that it becomes possible to then go to the top of the model and undertake customer acquisition programs in which acquired customers will look like your "best" current customers. Chapter 8 covers the steps in the top portion of the Integrated Marketing Model.

As was noted earlier, for a business to survive during the next decade, it must manage the communication with its internal and external customers at every possible point of contact and use the knowledge gained through those contacts to create value in the relationship. It is only through this that a community of customers can arise.

Notes

1. Philip Kotler, "Marketing's New Paradigm: What's Really Happening Out There," *Planning Review,* September–October 1992, 50.

2. Rudy Oetting and Geri Gantman, "Dial 'M' for Maximize," *Sales & Marketing Management,* June 1991, 106.

3. Robert C. Blattberg and John Deighton, "Interactive Marketing: Exploiting the Age of Addressability," *Sloan Management Review,* Fall 1991, 7.

4. Patricia Sellers, "Keeping the Buyers You Already Have," *Fortune,* Autumn/Winter 1993, 56.

5. Rahul Jacob, "Why Some Customers Are More Equal Than Others," *Fortune,* 12 September 1994, 218.

6. Lisa A. Petrison, Robert C. Blattberg, and Paul Wang, "Database Marketing: Past, Present, and Future," *Journal of Direct Marketing* 7:3, Summer 1991, 39.

7. Robert E. Wayland and Paul M. Cole, "Turn Customer Service Into Customer Profitability," *Management Review,* July 1994, 24.

8. Frederick F. Reichheld, "Loyalty-based Management," *Harvard Business Review,* March–April 1993, 66.

9. James L. Heskett, et al., "Putting the Service-Profit Chain to Work," *Harvard Business Review,* March–April 1994, 170.

10. Reichheld, 66.

11. Reichheld, 71.

12. Jacqueline Damian, "Does Your Company Pass or Fail Service?" *Electronics,* May 1991, 50.

13. John Goodman, Scott M. Broetzmann, and Dianne S. Ward, "Preventing TQM Problems: Measured Steps Toward Customer-Driven Quality Improvement," *National Productivity Review,* Autumn 1993, 556.

14. Goodman, Broetzmann, and Ward, 557.

15. Heskett, et al., 167.

16. Patricia Sellers, "What Customers Really Want," *Fortune,* 4 June 1990, 59.

17. Sellers, "What Customers Really Want," 59.

18. Sellers, "What Customers Really Want," 66–68.

19. Christopher W. L. Hart, James L. Heskett, and W. Earl Sasser, Jr.,
    "The Profitable Art of Service Recovery," *Harvard Business
    Review,* July–August 1990, 154.

20. Heskett, et al., 174.

21. William H. Davidow and Bro Uttal, *Total Customer Service: The
    Ultimate Weapon* (New York: Harper & Row), 1989, 94–95.

3

DETERMINING EXTERNAL SERVICE VALUES

The first step in building a customer community is understanding your customer. You need to know why a customer buys from you, how they buy, what they value in their relationship with you, and what you can do to further the relationship. External service values involve two basic issues—defining who the customer is and determining what unique product or service attributes drive each customer's purchasing behaviors. This is a fundamental marketing and economic concept many forget. To put it simply, you need to know specifically why customers, individually and as segments, buy from you.

The important point here is external service values— those things that are important to your customers—are directly connected to purchasing behavior, which is the ultimate measurement of the effectiveness of the relationship. By identifying those external service values the customer considers important in the purchasing decision, you begin laying the foundation for the community-building process.

Taking this a step further: since external service values are those product or service features/attributes that trigger purchasing behavior, they are the things differentiating your product/service from the competition. If you have the core competencies to provide these external service values, then you will have the competency and capacity to sustain satisfying customer needs, giving you a strong competitive advantage.

ASSESSING CUSTOMER NEEDS

The first step is to understand the customer's needs. Stephen Covey, in describing his "Seek first to understand" philosophy, stated, " 'Seek first to understand' involves a very deep shift in paradigm. Most people listen, not with intent to understand, but with the intent to reply. They're either speaking or preparing to speak."[1]

Covey goes on to say this leads to *empathetic* listening, which involves several steps:

- First, in order to understand another person, *you must be willing to be influenced.* This means abandoning fixed positions. You have to enter into the communication or dialogue with an attitude of being willing to change, if necessary. By doing this, you become more open.

- This openness leads to the second action, *giving people room to release their fixed position and consider alternatives.* When the other person realizes you are open to change, they will be more willing to consider options that previously conflicted with their fixed positions.

- The third aspect is, by seeking to understand, *you gain influence over the relationship.* That is, the customer allows you to be helpful to them, which moves the relationship closer to the spirit of community. If you take the time to understand what the customer's needs are, you can then address those needs with more appropriate offers or communication. Without this understanding, you are simply selling products. With it, you are offering solutions.

- Finally, seeking first to understand leads people to *discover the third alternative.* Now both engage, through dialogue, in a synergistic approach to problem solving, finding an alternative neither would have considered alone.

This leads to a key concept: *Meeting a customer s changing needs with the right solution at the right time is how value is created in the relationship.* If you have a means of listening to the customer, and you take action responsive to the customer, you are going to add value to the relationship. Much of this is accomplished through the new way in which you communicate with the customer—you first listen.

TYPES OF NEEDS

Before identifying external service values, a basic review of needs is required. Ted Levitt, the well-known marketing professor, addressed the topic of needs in his *Total Product Concept*: "A customer attaches value to a product in proportion to its perceived ability to help solve his problem or meet his needs."[2]

Levitt identified four product categories—generic, expected, augmented, and potential.

1. The generic product represents the basics in the marketplace. It is the minimum you have to provide in order to exist in a market.

2. The expected product is based on the customer's minimum expectations. It is what the customer considers absolutely essential in the purchasing decision. The generic product may satisfy the technical requirements of the purchase, but the expected product may involve aspects such as just-in-time delivery, extended credit terms or volume discounts, and on-site technical service support.[3] Levitt sees the interaction between these two product categories as, "The generic product can be sold only if the customer's wider expectations are met. Different means may be employed to meet those expectations. Hence differentiation follows expectations."[4]

3. The third product category is the augmented product. The augmented product exceeds the customer's expectations. This category is what differentiates one supplier from an-another. For example, if a computer manufacturer includes an imbedded diagnostic tool in a product, this augments the expected product offering. However, Levitt warns, "Not all customers for all products and under all circumstances, however, can be attracted by an ever-expanding

bundle of differentiating value satisfactions. Some customers may prefer lower prices to product augmentation. Some cannot use the extra services offered."[5]

4. Levitt defines the fourth product category as, "Everything that might be done to attract and hold customers is what can be called the potential product."[6]

Levitt's categories reflect the principles of building a customer community. Through continuously monitoring and measuring the customer relationship, you identify the generic and expected product needs. From these, you can then develop augmented and potential products to differentiate your product or service offerings from the competition.

IDENTIFYING CUSTOMER/MARKET NEEDS

A logical law of marketing is customers have three levels of needs: basic, unfulfilled, and future.

Basic Needs

Basic needs are those that must be met before the customer will consider the product or service offering. Levitt uses a poker analogy, explaining that meeting basic needs are the table stakes to get into the game. These are the product or service features everyone offers. If all competitors in a market only fulfill basic needs, you have a commodity product.

However, the term "commodity products" is a bit of a misnomer in today's highly competitive markets. As Levitt puts it: "There is no such thing as a commodity. All goods and services are differentiable. . . . In the marketplace, differentiation is everywhere. Everybody—producer, fabricator, seller, broker, agent, merchant—tries constantly to distinguish his offering from all others. This is true even of those who produce and deal in primary metals, grains, chemicals, plastics, and money."[7]

Unfulfilled Needs

Determining and then meeting the customer's unfulfilled needs enables you to differentiate your product or service, which gives you a competitive advantage. Unfulfilled needs fall into three categories. The first, and most obvious, category includes those customer needs neither you nor your competition are currently satisfying. If you can find a way to satisfy these needs, you have the opportunity to dominate the market segment. Yet, remember these are unfulfilled *customer* needs. This is not a case of randomly "tacking" more features onto a product. The *feature* must *benefit* a customer *need*. If the need doesn't exist, neither does the benefit or fulfillment of a need.

A second type of unfulfilled need is the one your competitor is satisfying and you are not. Unless you can satisfy this need on a sustainable basis, i.e., have the core competencies to fulfill the need, this customer will be at risk. If this is a current customer, you may find your relationship increasingly more costly and less satisfying.

The third unfulfilled need type is the one neither you nor your competitors are aware of or able to act on. These unknown needs represent a unique opportunity if you can uncover them. That is where the importance of community becomes apparent: the only way to discover this kind of need is to continually monitor changing customer circumstances.

Future Needs

Knowing current unfulfilled needs leads naturally into the ability to anticipate future needs. For example, if you are marketing to OEMs, you want to be aware of products they are developing. If you have developed a relationship with the customer, you will recognize these needs. Future needs help you to align yourself strategically, but have little short-term value since they do not drive successful lead generation programs. You also need to determine if your core competencies will support fulfilling these future needs.

DEFINING EXTERNAL SERVICE VALUES

Unless, and until, you know what causes the individual customer to buy from you, you cannot effectively market your product. Three steps can be used to uncover and define potential external service values. They can be discrete for a customer segment, or shared among several segments. Typically, between four and seven external service values will define 80 percent of the purchasing behavior in most segments.

Ask the Customer

The first step is the simplest: ask the customer. To many, this sounds too simplistic, but it works. After the customer purchases your product, call them, thank them, and ask them what influenced them to buy your product rather than someone else's. This will help you identify some basic categories of potential external service values.

Talk to Defectors

The second approach—talking with those customers who have defected—is important for two reasons. First, it will help you identify other potential at-risk customers. Second, you can better focus your resources. Defectors will tell you what customer need you failed to satisfy. In turn, you can analyze these unfulfilled needs to determine if they are important to other customers.

For example, if some customers defect because of delayed delivery—and that is an important external service value to other existing customers—then you risk losing other customers if you do not improve delivery as an external service value. Uncovering deficiencies before they adversely affect your existing customer base is critical for continued success. It also aids you in selecting the type of customer you want to attract.

This is not to say you want to "save" all defectors. Rather, you have a rational basis for deciding who to do business with, namely those customers whose needs match your core competencies or ability to fulfill those needs.

Glenn DeSouza, president of Strategic Quality Systems, Inc., identified six types of defectors:

1. Price defectors who defect to a low-priced competitor.

2. Product defectors are those who leave for a better product. While a price customer can be recovered, someone who has

switched because of a technically-superior product may not be recoverable.

3. Service defectors are dissatisfied with the service.

4. Market defectors are customers who have gone out of business or have moved out of your market area.

5. Technology defectors move to new technology from outside your market segment. For example, some dedicated word processor manufacturers did not recognize the threat from PC technology and subsequently lost their market to the new technology.

6. Organizational defectors leave because of internal or external political concerns. For example, a company like Boeing encounters problems with foreign airlines that are state-owned.[8]

These helpful categories can be used when analyzing customers-at-risk. Obviously, some categories are not salvageable. Therefore, the second advantage of talking with defectors is you can better focus your resources, rather than misapplying them to try to save customers you are going to lose anyway.

Feature Set Profile

The third approach in determining external service values is the Feature Set Profile, a five-step process that causes you to scrutinize the entire range of your product or service offerings, match those with your competitors', and compare them with your customer's needs.

1. Attribute/feature analysis. The first step is to develop a comprehensive list of all your product or service features and attributes. This should be an inclusive list ranging from specific product features to all the services wrapped around the product. Typically this list is from 50 to 120 items.

For example, a list for a laptop computer manufacturer might include product features such as CPU, disk drives, software, and so on—all aspects of the physical product. Then it might include external features such as design, packaging, case colors, etc. Another category could be manufacturer operational attributes including shipping time, quote generation, billing, etc. Another area could be marketing, including volume discounts, special offers, order fulfillment, warranties, etc.

2. Competitive analysis. Once you have completed your feature/attribute list, compare each with what your competition has to offer. This is critical because, unless you know how you compare with the competition, you will not be aware of those attributes that set you apart from the competition.

Sometimes it is difficult to make valid competitive comparisons, but this analysis provides a range of criteria to define critical competitive issues. It's critical that you look beyond price, physical product, and features. Kevin McGarrity, a vice president at Texas Instruments and director of worldwide sales and marketing noted: "What's happened is that all the global pressure that we and our customers are now facing has required that we step back and take a fresh look at how we stay competitive beyond the traditional buy-and-sell relationship. And what we've found is that a lot of the elements of customer satisfaction have to do with other issues beyond cost."[9]

3. Undifferentiated features. Those features/attributes you and your competition offer at equal levels can be considered undifferentiated features. These are the "table stakes" you need to get into the game. These features do not cause differentiated purchasing behaviors. Since everyone in the market offers these, the customer has no reason to select one supplier over another to fulfill the basic needs.

4. Identify competitive differences. After the undifferentiated features have been identified, analyze the list to determine those features/attributes in which you excel, or you offer and your competition does not. These form the core list of your potential external service values, or unique attributes.

Hopefully, you will end up with a set of features no one else is delivering. For example, from an original list of one hundred items, you may find ten are items no one else offers. Figure 3-1 shows part of a feature set profile.

Feature	Our company	Competitor Two	Competitor Three	Competitor Four
Time to ship	48 hours	48 hours	5 days	Same day
Guarantee	Unlimited	60	120	90
Handling charge	No	No	Yes	No
Quote turnaround	4 hours	2 days	24 hours	N/A
Volume pricing	Yes	Yes	Yes	Yes
Accuracy of order fulfillment	100%	98%	95%	100%
Recycled packaging	No	No	No	No
Price guarantee	90 days	No	30 days	No
Toll-free number	Yes	Yes	Yes	Yes
Customizing	5–10 days	6 weeks	5 weeks	No

Figure 3-1 Feature Set Profile

The Feature Set Profile shows a select number of features and compares them with competitive features. In this example, guarantee, quote turnaround, price guarantee, and customizing would appear to be potential external service values.

Of course, the corollary to this is that any features/attributes your competition excels in, or features your competition offers and you do not, potentially put your customers at risk if they value that feature. These become competitive offerings that may put you at a disadvantage. In this example, the time to ship attribute may be in this category.

However, keep in mind, at this point of the process only internal information is being used. The list is based on internal analyses and perceptions. These are the features/attributes *you* think make a difference.

5. Talk with your customer. After identifying your unique feature set, test it with your customers. Here you verify these attributes are indeed the ones customers or a target market segment believe fulfill a need, drive purchasing behavior, and build a relationship.

Several methods can be used to determine what attributes the customer values in their purchasing decision. One method is to conduct a survey through the mail or by phone. The other is to conduct a focus group with select customers. Remember, since each segment has different needs, they will value different features.

RANK-ORDER NEEDS

Whichever method you use, you want customers to rank-order the list of unique attributes based on the value to them. Rank-ordering attributes gives you a means of segmenting customers by common sets of needs. For example, when grouping customers together that have the same needs, you will often find they have similar attributes, such as functional title, size of company, type of industry, etc. These then become the selectable attributes you can use to define segments.

In addition to rank-ordering, ask customers how important each is in terms of buying. For example, in the worst case, they may rank-order the list of unique attributes, but indicate none are important to their buying decision. In the best case, several attributes will be identified as important to their buying behavior. These may qualify as external service values. Figure 3-2 shows rank-ordering for the Feature Set Profile in Figure 3-1.

Unique Features	Rank-Order	Importance
Guarantee	3	1
Quote turnaround	2	4
Price guarantee	1	5
Customizing	4	2

1 = low 5 = high

Figure 3-2 Rank-Order Features

In this example, customer rank-ordering and, more importantly, importance show that price guarantee and quote turnaround are external service values for this category or customer segment. Don't forget, for these to be sustainable, they must be supported by core competencies.

Focusing on purchasing behavior first, then on building long-term relationships, seems simple. But it is at the heart of what the customer values.

For example, a computer supply catalog company discovered 80 percent of their target market considered only two sources for supplies and 40 percent bought from their hardware manufacturer. By refocusing on their hardware-installed base, the company more than doubled the effectiveness of their program.

Once you have identified the external service values for a segment, you then need to reinforce those in all communication with the customer. It should be reemphasized here that these external service values are at the core of your marketing effort to the related segment. They not only set you apart from the competition, but more importantly, they are responsible for a customer's purchasing behavior and become the foundation for a sustainable relationship. When you become aware of your external service values, you can then direct your resources toward enhancing them to not only satisfy the customer, but to delight them.

NEEDS AT RISK

As was mentioned previously, the first order of business is current business, i.e., meeting the current needs of your customers. Unmet needs will put your customer relationship at risk. The first step in identifying at-risk situations is to conduct a customer needs assessment. Through this, you need to become sensitive to unmet needs as they are harbingers of customer defections.

As you attempt to uncover and understand customer needs, you have to take care during the process. First, you need to ensure you are listening to understand the customer's needs and not projecting your biases on the process. In other words, "seek first to understand."

Second, you need to accurately interpret the information you get from the customer. Francis Gouillart and Frederick Sturdivant, senior vice presidents of Gemini Consulting Group, made this point when they noted: "Customers can describe their experiences and define their immediate needs. But only you can interpret their data and help them solve their problems. Being market focused is about your own creativity uncovering and solving your customers' problems."[10]

It may seem contradictory, but, at times, you need to discount what the customer says. A *Fortune* article noted, "Ignore what your customers say; pay attention to what they do."[11]

That's a key concept—*pay attention to what the customer does*. In building a community of customers you carefully track customer behavior; in other words, you pay attention to what the customer actually does. You do this through the four basic measurements—recency, frequency, purchase amount, and referrals. Those measurements will tell you what is really important to your customers and provide the criteria you need to determine how well the customer's needs match your ability to deliver.

IDENTIFYING CORE COMPETENCIES

It is one thing to identify needs and external service values. It is another to be able to sustain the delivery of those values. To be sustainable, the external service values must be supported by core competencies within your organization. Core competencies are defined as "the technologies, specialized expertise, business processes and techniques that a company has accumulated over time and packaged in its offerings."[12]

Identifying core competencies can be a key in deciding which kinds of business to pursue. If the customer has an unfulfilled need, you may not be able to competitively satisfy that need unless that ability is part of your core competency.

Here's one such example. A company wanted to tap into the PC supply market. They determined shipping orders within twenty-four hours had unique value to the customer. However, the company's culture and processes were geared to batch processing of orders, where all parts of the order came together for one delivery. The best they could do was ship orders every nine days. Therefore, their core competency did not match the potential customer's needs and did not support a critical external service value. The result was, since they were unable to meet customers' needs for timely delivery, they abandoned this segment of the business.

Michael Treacy and Fred Wiersema believe a company must excel in one or more core competencies, which they label *value disciplines*. Their studies concluded a company needs to excel in one of three areas—operational excellence, customer intimacy, and product leadership—and meet the industry standard in the other two.[13]

In the area of *operational excellence*, the authors cite GE's Direct Connection program as an example. Through this program, GE redefined how it does business with independent appliance retailers. These retailers had faced a dual threat— from large chain stores' low-price marketing and from appliance manufacturers who expected dealers to carry a full inventory. The latter obviously added inventory costs, which made the retailer even less competitive with the volume discount chains.

Not wanting to lose the independent retailer as a distribution channel, GE completely changed the way in which they did business with the retailer. Rather than require the retailer to carry a full inventory, GE now, through the Direct Connection program, provides the dealer with a "virtual" inventory. Participating retailers use a twenty-four-hour computer system to check on the inventory of hundreds of ranges, refrigerators, and other appliances. The retailer has a limited store inventory of display models. The customer is assured quick delivery. And the retailer does not tie up capital in inventory and becomes more competitive.

In exchange, the retailer has a commitment to carry a specific number of GE appliance lines and has some financial commitments, including having GE products account for at least 50 percent of sales. An added benefit is that now GE can track actual sales, rather than "inventory" sales to retailers. This gives GE more accurate market data.[14]

This is a good example of delivering external service value. In this case, GE is meeting unfulfilled needs of the independent retailer. And, it is meeting those needs with a core competency. GE has the experience in warehousing, inventory management, and delivery that an independent retailer may lack. By taking on these responsibilities for the retailer, GE gains in retailer retention and loyalty.

The second value discipline Treacy and Wiersema discuss is *customer intimacy*. Their definition of this parallels the description of customer community. In essence, they are saying you continually fine-tune your product or service to meet the needs of an increasingly finite customer universe. The community approach identifies the needs of the individual customer and meets those needs through new or enhanced product or services. Then, logical groupings of like-minded customers become market segments.

The third value discipline, *product leadership*, involves a complex set of criteria. First, companies have to be innovative. But creativity is not enough. Companies have to be able to quickly take new ideas and bring them to market. In today's fast-paced competitive world, windows of opportunity quickly close.[15]

This, again, closely parallels the concepts of customer community. It summarizes what an analysis of external service values produces. By focusing on the unfulfilled needs, as perceived by customers, and having the core competencies to fulfill those needs, *you in effect are defining your business and the type of customer you want to do business with*.

SEGMENTING MARKETS USING EXTERNAL SERVICE VALUES

External service values also provide a more precise means of segmenting markets. Most companies segment around industries and then look at application needs. For example, industry segments may include retailing, manufacturing, government, health care, etc.

This produces extremely rough, or gross, segmentation. The next step would be to look at application needs within each industry segment. A company like Toshiba may take manufacturing and segment its applications such as sales automation, financial, etc.

This still gives you a granular form of segmentation. However, if you take each of these application areas and further segment along common external service values, you are further narrowing the segments and honing in on the factors that drive purchasing behaviors. Using the Toshiba example, but segmenting on sales force automation, you could easily cut across many SIC groups. An external service value could be turnkey software application installation and training.

Segmentation allows you to communicate with a group about subjects they will identify to be of interest and value to them. This approach identifies a relatively small number of subjects, or external service values, for each segment and, therefore, greatly simplifies personalization of your communication.

It is the process of determining the external service values, which are built on common sets of unfulfilled needs, matched core competencies, and similar purchasing behaviors, that drives segmentation and target marketing. The logical next step is to find out how you can communicate these values to the customer.

COMMUNITY BUILDING IN ACTION: BUSINESSFORMS*

BusinessForms is a division of a large printing company specializing in customized business forms. Like many business-to-business marketers, its distribution channels include field sales, distributors, third-party resellers, and direct catalog sales. Its products, which are near-generic or commodity-types, cut across industries and require nonproduct differentiation to be competitive.

*Note: BusinessForms is a fictitious company based on client experiences. We will be using it here and in subsequent chapters to help illustrate the topics covered in each chapter.

Background

In the early 1980s BusinessForms was a product-focused marketer producing traditional sheet-fed forms. With the advent of computer software packages and pin-fed printers to handle computer-generated forms, management believed an opportunity existed for customized forms designed to work with specific software packages. In this way, the software users would have forms that incorporated their logo and other graphics.

Original analysis revealed that computer-generated forms are different from sheet-fed forms. To be successful in this field, the BusinessForms division learned that pin alignment with the form and preprinted layouts are critical. So their focus was to develop products that met those needs.

During the process of developing their business plan, the company learned accounting software was the biggest user of computer-generated forms. In this field, a handful of software companies dominated the market, and forming some type of alliance with software publishers was the best strategy for penetrating the market. So the division approached the software companies and offered, in exchange for their customer list, to pay the companies a royalty on all sales generated from their customers.

In these initial efforts, BusinessForms relied on direct mail and telemarketing as the primary sales channel. They would first contact the prospect by phone, further qualify their needs, send a product catalog, and then follow up to close the sale.

As reps talked with prospects, they found that the major competitor was not other national forms companies, but local printers. Some customers liked to have face-to-face support. The reps also learned some of these companies were using their accountants for turnkey solutions, which included using one of the accounting software packages on the market. So, the division began developing alliances with accounting firms, which supplied them with the customer name. BusinessForms sold direct to the customer, and the accounting firm received a royalty from each sale.

As the company continued to learn more about its customers, it discovered other companies were providing turnkey solutions. These typically were value-added resellers (VARs) and other third-party suppliers. In this case, the VARs wanted the forms supplied to them, which enabled them to add further value in their customer relationships. So the division set up a separate distribution arm to exclusively sell to VARs and other third parties.

Moving from Product to Channel Focus

At this point, the company began to consider expanding its product offerings, moving from a product focus to a functional focus and different distribution channels.

As the division grew their computer-generated forms business, they analyzed their customer base to see if current customers needed other forms besides accounting-related ones.

When customers were asked what other forms they used, most people were not sure how to describe specific forms. So the rep would ask the customer to provide a sample of every form used in their business. The rep then arranged to have the sample forms picked up by UPS at no cost to the customer. Quotes would be prepared for each type of form, and then in a follow-up call the telemarketer would discuss the quotes and, hopefully, close the sale.

While this process seemed to work better, some customer indecision and confusion remained. So the division began putting salespeople into the field to pick up the forms and hand-deliver the quotes. But there was a problem: this was not an economical way for all customers since the average lifetime value of some customers did not justify two face-to-face sales calls. Yet, face-to-face selling was important with key accounting firms.

So a compromise solution was developed: the forms were picked up from most end users by UPS, but the field sales representative delivered the quote. This enabled the field sales representative to answer customer questions, revise quotes, and provide other information. Following this initial call by the field sales representative, future contact with the customer was handled by telemarketing and direct mail. Similar economic models were built for each sales channel.

As this process developed, the company moved closer and closer to understanding customers' needs, which were defined by industry as much as by business functions. For example, beyond the simple distinction between computer or pin-fed forms and non-computer forms, customers in different industries had radically different forms needs. A manufacturing company and a health care provider had different form requirements.

Next, the division began to segment their market by industry categories with similar sets of needs. In their case, they defined three vertical segments—manufacturing, health care, and government—that had common sets of needs.

Once they took this approach, they discovered each vertical market had subsegments, each with its own set of needs. For example, they identified fourteen subsegments, such as large hospitals, veterinarians, and dentists, within the health care segment.

What the division did was to get down to identifying needs at the individual customer level. These needs had been defined initially by the type of forms used, but as reps developed relationships with customers, they were able to discover a greater amount of details. From this, they were able to develop common sets of needs into target market segments.

One of these "details" involved the individual customer buying procedures. For example, some hospitals' buying procedures are centralized, others are decentralized. This may apply to a single hospital or a group of hospitals. How a hospital buys has an impact on who the company sells to and how it sells. Again, this is dependent upon the customer's stated needs.

Figure 3-3 gives a visual depiction of the health care market showing the thirteen vertical subsegments along with the buying process.

While this segmentation has dramatically gone beyond the simplistic pin-fed forms and other forms segmentation, it still represents a relatively "rough cut" at segmentation based on customer needs. The company's dental segments are an example.

Determining External Service Values

First the division separated solo dental practices from group practices. They then developed a Feature Set Profile (Figure 3-4). The division first listed all its product and service attributes. It then determined competitive features and attributes.

After they analyzed competitive offerings in each category, the division had a grid similar to Figure 3-4.

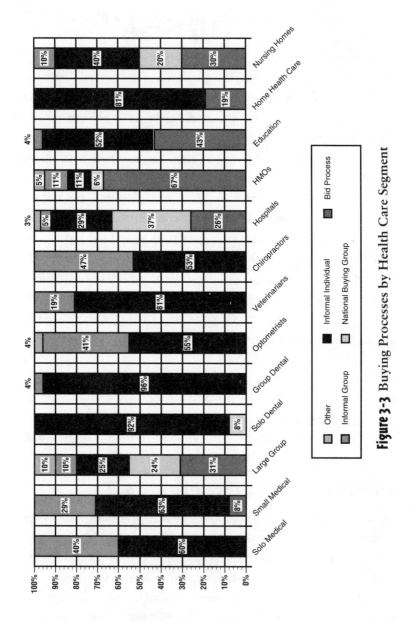

Figure 3-3 Buying Processes by Health Care Segment

Feature	Our company	Competitor Two	Competitor Three	Competitor Four
Time to ship	Same day	2 days	5 days	Same day
Guarantee	Unlimited	60	120	90
Handling charge	No	No	Yes	No
Quote turnaround	4 hours	2 days	24 hours	N/A
Volume pricing	Yes	Yes	Yes	Yes
Accuracy of order fulfillment	100%	98%	95%	100%
Recycled packaging	No	No	No	No
Price guarantee	90 days	No	30 days	No
Toll-free number	Yes	Yes	Yes	Yes
Customizing	5–10 days	6 weeks	5 weeks	No

Figure 3-4 Feature Set Profile

In Figure 3-4, volume pricing and toll-free numbers are offered by everyone. Guarantee and time to customize offer potential unique benefits. Going to the customer to confirm purchasing behavior around these features, and examining the ability to provide that feature, leads to external service values.

Having identified a common set of needs, they stressed these in literature and other communication with the customer in that subsegment.

The results from this type of approach can be stunning. One company saw their total market potential blossom. They identified a new market that bought the same way their customers did and valued the same service/features. This resulted in a 300 percent increase in the target market size of those who looked like and behaved like their existing customers!

Notes

1. Stephen R. Covey, *The 7 Habits of Highly Effective People* (New York: Simon and Schuster 1989), 239.

2. Theodore Levitt, "Marketing Success Through Differentiation—of Anything," *Harvard Business Review,* January–February 1980, 84–85.

3. Levitt, 85–87.

4. Levitt, 87.

5. Levitt, 87.

6. Levitt, 88.

7. Levitt, 83.

8. Glenn DeSouza, "Designing a Customer Retention Plan," *The Journal of Business Strategy,* March/April 1992, 25–26.

9. Samuel Weber, "It's a Whole New Way of Doing Business" *Electronics,* July 1990, 55.

10. Francis J. Gouillart and Frederick D. Sturdivant, "Spend a Day in the Life of Your Customers," *Harvard Business Review,* January–February 1994, 123.

11. Justin Martin, "Ignore Your Customer," *Fortune,* 1 May 1995, 126.

12. Richard Normann and Rafael Ramirez, "From the Value Chain to Value Constellation: Designing Interactive Strategy," *Harvard Business Review,* July–August 1993, 74.

13. Michael Treacy and Fred Wiersema, "Customer Intimacy and Other Value Disciplines," *Harvard Business Review,* January–February 1993, 84.

14. Treacy and Wiersema, 86–87.

15. Treacy and Wiersema, 90.

4

COMMUNICATING WITH YOUR CUSTOMER

Contacts—communications with both internal and external customers—are information pathways. *Whoever owns these vital pathways, owns the relationship with the customer.* They deliver value, based on what is considered valuable by the customer.

In business-to-business marketing, the focus is on servicing and managing relationships with customers in the overall sales and marketing process. It is economically important to use the most effective contact medium—mail, or phone, or fax, or field sales, or space advertising. But, it is vitally important that each contact's content delivers value. This is what contributes to building relationships that lead to customer loyalty.

Who determines which contacts are important? The customer does. It is the customer who determines which contact delivers value to them, the content of that contact, the timing, the medium, and the frequency of the contacts. These become building blocks in this new customer community.

COMMUNICATING VALUE

The external service values that you developed for the customer drive the communication content of your contacts with the customer. The first step in the process of understanding how to communicate external service values to the customer—no matter which contact medium is used—is to reexamine the selling process.

The classic "spray and pray" model does not work in today's economy. Customers and prospects alike are becoming less tolerant of valueless contacts. These build up a behavior of "anti-phone call" and "anti-mail" that, in business marketing, you cannot afford. You have a finite universe of potential customers. To vaccinate these individuals with valueless contacts pricks them until they scab over—inoculating them to your message even when you do have something of value to deliver.

Classic Selling Myths

The classic, or traditional, model of selling is centered on face-to-face contact. Its basis is that face-to-face is the essential part of the selling process and regularly required by the customer to do business. What this classic approach has not recognized are the alternatives to, or ways to leverage, face-to-face that can be just as effective, or more effective at a lower cost, *and* often preferred by the customer.

One of the ironies of selling is sales representatives often consider face-to-face contact the most important part of the selling process. Yet, as previously cited studies have shown, customers often prefer mail, or a combination of mail and phone contact, over face-to-face contact. They don't have the time to devote to face-to-face contact unless that contact delivers unique value.

The myths based on the traditional selling model include:

1. Close the order: The inherent belief is face-to-face selling is necessary to close the order. It focuses on the event, or the sale, rather than on providing solutions.

2. Productive use of time: Another myth is field salespeople make productive use of their time.

3. Personality sells: The old paradigm was that the salesperson's personality was a key factor in the selling process.

4. New business is the key: Sales representatives too often are measured on their ability to attract new business.

Disadvantages of the Classic Model

The disadvantages of the classic selling model are that it is too costly, not productive, and often not competitive:

1. IBM does not need face-to-face to sell an add-on AS400 disk drive, which may cost thousands of dollars. The customers know when they need additional disk space and they can simply call with the order or be contacted by IBM Telesales.

2. Studies show salespeople often spend too much time with low-potential customers, not enough time with top-performing customers, no time with low-potential customers, or too much time with top-performing customers.

3. The old-time, glad-hand routine—with tickets to the ball game and long lunches with congenial stories—is dead. Buyers and purchasing agents do not have the time to spend in nonproductive endeavors. More and more buying decisions are being made by committees or end users. With the emphasis on productivity and lower overall costs at all levels of the organization, these key influencers no longer succumb to personality selling. They are looking for solutions, not free lunches.

4. The classic approach tends to encourage salespeople to chase unqualified leads just because they happen to be in the geographic area of the lead. This is nonproductive and steals time from cultivating and nurturing existing customers.

The new role of the salesperson is fast becoming more of a consultant or problem-solver than the traditional "peddler." This new role requires focusing on understanding the customer and providing value, which often takes the form of advice or counsel. As product differentiation becomes more costly, services often become economic salvation.

At this point, an interesting question arises: Is this "advice" free? Of course not. Typically, the cost is loaded into the product. It becomes a "value-added" service, or external service value, in the business relationship.

A NEW SALES PARADIGM

Frequent Face-to-Face Is Not Essential

Face-to-face contact has unique and unduplicated roles to fulfill in the overall sales process. Certain aspects of interaction with customers, such as inventory management, training, product demonstrations, and on-site audits of activities, are best accomplished with face-to-face contact.

However, various studies show customers are shifting their preference away from face-to-face contact to immediate access. For example, the previously cited Arthur Andersen study (Figure 4-1) shows contact with the outside salesperson has dropped in order of importance from first to eighth, while access to a capable inside salesperson (i.e., immediate access) has risen to be the most preferred contact medium.

Service	1970	1980	1985	1990
Contact with outside salesperson	First	Third	Fifth	Eighth
Frequency and speed of delivery	Second	First	First	Second
Price	Third	Second	Third	Fourth
Range of available products	Fourth	Fifth	Fourth	Third
Capable inside salesperson	Fifth	Fourth	Second	First

Figure 4-1 Customer Contact Preferences

Source: Based on Arthur Andersen & Co. data.

A recent confidential study confirms this from a different perspective. The study, conducted by a $2.2 billion company, found 50 percent of their customers, five days after a contact, *could not recall whether the contact was face-to-face or by phone.* Think about that for a moment. *Five days after being contacted, the person cannot recall how the contact was made, but can recall the content of the contact.* And, for this company, face-to-face contact cost them $460, while a phone contact cost $18.

The Shell experience with contact frequency. To further illustrate this, consider Team TBA's experience. At the time Team TBA was set up to market Shell's batteries, tires, and accessories, Shell had sixty-seven field sales personnel dedicated to this business. This was reduced to seventeen field representatives by significantly decreasing personal sales calls with a concurrent dramatic increase in telephone and mail contacts. This resulted in a multimillion dollar savings in sales costs.

After twelve months, in a survey of Shell service stations, customers were asked what they thought about the level of service they were getting. In thirty of thirty-one service/satisfaction categories, perceived levels increased. Many of the respondents stated they were very satisfied but knew Team TBA couldn't continue the high level of contact because it was too expensive. Yet, there had been *a significant reduction in contact costs per dealer.*

More suprising was the perceived frequency of field sales contact. Despite a 75 percent reduction in salespeople and face-to-face contacts per dealer, the integration of mail, phone, and field contacts actually created a perceived *increase* of 17 percent in field contact frequency.

These studies and the Shell experience clearly demonstrate the customer is less concerned with the contact medium than with the content. Contact *content*—i.e., value—is more important than contact *medium* and, of course, perceived value increases with the frequency of *value-based* contact. The key term here is *value-based contact*, which does not mean randomly contacting customers with just any message. That would be like throwing spaghetti against the wall and hoping some sticks. Rather, it involves a periodic contact plan of valued communication that has frequency of contact as one of its characteristics.

Two key terms come into play here: *efficiency* and *effectiveness*. Efficiency has to do with the cost of the event. The lowest cost for an activity is the most efficient. Effectiveness has to do with producing a desired effect, in this case, purchasing behavior. The most efficient contact medium may not be the most effective. The new sales paradigm embraces the best of both concepts, leveraging the high cost of personal contact with other, lower-cost, contact media to provide the highest value to the customer and most cost-effective approach for selling.

Future Revenue Determines Potential

In the new sales paradigm, the future revenue stream for each customer—not the size of yesterday's order—determines the potential of the customer. First determine how valuable the individual customer is and then use this as the basis for an economic model that identifies the type and frequency of contact the customer can support.

For example, BusinessForms determined the average lifetime value of their dental market is $1,075. Obviously, if their cost for a face-to-face sales contact is $350, then it does not make economic sense to have a salesperson call on this level of customer. However, if the top tier of customers for this company has a lifetime value ten or twenty times the average, there's then economic justification to use a salesperson in the selling process.

The key is to pay attention to the economics of selling as well as to what you are selling. For some of your customers, there may be a set of activities, such as face-to-face contact, that are not economically justified based on the revenue stream from their purchases. The account management/contact plan developed later in this chapter shows how revenue impacts the level of contact that can economically be applied to a customer.

Loyalty as a Sales Goal

Revenue is an important measure, but it is only one. Most companies establish sales goals around revenues, yet sales statistics do not directly measure the value of a customer base or any change in the value. Rather, sales figures are a gross dollar measure of a customer's purchasing behavior over a fixed period of time. Lifetime value, on the other hand, is an asset measure.

Lifetime value of a customer also is a measure of loyalty. A "loyal customer" is one who consistently purchases from you, increases their breadth of purchases, and refers you to other potential customers. Loyal customers provide a threefold benefit:

- Since they buy from you, rather than having to be sold, your marketing and sales costs are lower.

- Since you have a relationship with the customers, you know a great deal about them and don't have to expend resources on transactions such as credit checking, account setup, returns, etc.

- Loyal customers buy more in terms of product or service depth and breadth.[1]

New Business Is More Than Cold Calling

A core issue of the new sales paradigm is that the first way to get new business is at the individual level from existing customers. To do this, first look to your current customer base for ways to sell more product lines to the individual existing customer and then look for ways to sell to more individuals within the customer's organization. This is truly new business development; i.e., "cultivating" your customer base, which becomes the foundation for low-cost sales revenue growth.

Then, when you do go after new customers, you base that upon the cultivation process. You want to find other customers that look like your sustainable or best customers. Finding the right prospects is the crucial aspect of effective new business acquisition. If you go after the wrong prospects, you are wasting valuable resources.

As marketing consultant and author Regis McKenna pointed out, ". . . many companies fail to realize that which customers they attract is often more important than how many customers they attract."[2]

UNDERSTANDING COMMUNICATION NEEDS

This new sales paradigm starts with communication. To understand a specific customer's communication needs—what the customer values in communication—ask customers what types of information they want in each type of contact, what contact medium they prefer, when they want to be contacted, and how often they want to be contacted. In other words, ask the customer to define their communication preferences.

This process is the key to understanding the customer's communication needs. Without it you will be unable to deliver value-based communications, which are needed in building a sustainable relationship with the customer.

Identify Each Contact Point

The first step in the process involves analyzing each point of contact with the customer. That is, what media are used to contact the customer and what media does the customer use to contact you.

Start your analysis by creating a log of all contact points and who "owns," or is responsible for, communication at that point. This admittedly detailed and time-consuming process will enable you to potentially manage those points of contact for value. Typically, you will find the customer contacts several different people within an organization. For example, the customer may contact your accounting department to get answers to billing questions, your shipping department to check on the status of an order, and your marketing department to request literature.

Once you have established all contact points, you need to have the people at those points diligently record each contact with a customer. It's best to record or sample at least 60 days of activity. Figure 4-2 shows a sample form:

Department (Group):	Key Contact:		Approvals:			
Time Period						
Activity	Phone		Mail		Electronic	
	In	Out	In	Out	In	Out
A. Sales/Revenue generation						
1. Orders/applications						
2. Contracts/confirmations/modifications						
B. Requests/exchange of information						
1. Product information						
2. Pricing/bid requests						
3. Literature/material						
4. Account related						
5. Special programs						
6. Other:						
C. Problems/customer service						
1. Shipment/completion status						
2. Problems/complaints						
3. Account corrections/adjustments						
4. Service related						
D. Messages/transfers						
E. Prospect/lead identification (solicited)						
F. Invoices/payments/claims/purchase orders						
G. Misdirected contacts/referrals						
H. Other:						

Figure 4-2 Sample Contact Log

© Hunter Business Direct, Inc.

Once you have compiled the individual contact logs, you consolidate and organize them on a spreadsheet. This produces a spreadsheet of contact activity counts for each contact point.

Often it is helpful to create two types of contact summaries—location and function. The first lists contacts by location and the second lists them by common function. Location allows analysis of similar functions done at the same location that may be more efficient if consolidated. Function allows looking across multiple locations to also consolidate for efficiency.

Figure 4-3 shows an abbreviated form of this analysis for inbound contacts in which the contact medium is also defined within each function. This has more detailed functional areas than shown on the sample contact log (Figure 4-2). It enables you to better plan for consolidation when designing and structuring the Customer Community Center.

Identifying Customer Preferences

The contact log gives you the first important insight on how and why customers have contacted you and how and why you have contacted them. This tells you what has happened. Armed with this information, you can now go to customers and ask them how, when, and why they *want* contact with you—what they want to happen.

When asking customers, first determine which type of contact medium the customer prefers for specific types of information. Then, identify how often they want each type of information during a year. For example, some customers may want to receive new product information through the mail.

Others may want new product information more quickly, by fax or phone. And others may prefer a face-to-face explanation by a salesperson.

If you understand how the customer wants to receive certain types of information and then deliver it to them in that manner, it *adds value to your relationship with the customer.*

Function	Location 1	Location 2	Location 3	Location 4	Location 5
1. Research					
External customer research		•			•
Needs assessment	•	•	•	•	•
Attribute profiles	•		•	•	
2. Assist with Planning					
Strategic insights from customer contact	•	•		•	•
Expense to revenue	•			•	
Mrktg. communications—value-based contacts		•			•
3. Leverage and Support Field Sales Force					
Handle customer service and billing problems	•	•	•	•	•
4. Function as Stand-alone Sales Channel					
Close sales	•		•	•	
Sell products/services	•		•	•	
Enter the order	•	•	•	•	•
Fulfill		•			•
Customer service	•		•	•	
5. Improve Productivity					
Make continuous improvement		•			•
6. Assimilate New Customers					
Thank them for their business					
Resolve problems	•	•	•	•	•

Figure 4-3 Function and Location Contact Analysis

© Hunter Business Direct, Inc.

VALUE-BASED CONTACT WORKSHOP

One way of getting this information is to invite a group of customers within a particular segment to participate in a value-based contact workshop. The main objective is to discover customer preferences by defining what they perceive is valuable information, how they prefer to receive that information, and how frequently they want to receive it. In addition to customers, the workshop includes a team of salespeople, both field and phone, and a team of marketing or product managers. Resellers may be included among the salespeople.

At the beginning of the workshop, review the contact log with all participants. Show them the types of contact that have been recorded. Have them discuss and define the content in each. At this stage, the primary concern is content and the desire to increase the value of your communication.

During the workshop, do the following:

1. Review the contact log. Focus on content and a new way of doing business.

2. Have each team meet among themselves and determine the types of content they believe are the most valuable in building a long-term, sustainable business relationship. Ask them to group these into ten categories and then rank-order them.

3. Have teams post their lists and explain why each item is on the list.

4. Reconcile the differences between each group and create a new list.

This process enables the customer, in conjunction with you, to define the value-basis of the relationship. This is a significant departure from most marketing planning, which focuses on the company's perceptions of what is valuable information in the relationship. Here, the customer defines information that has value for them.

BUILDING A CONTACT MODEL

Once a consensus has been developed, ask the customer how frequently they want to receive each content type. From this you can develop a value-based contact plan. Figure 4-4 shows a one-year contact plan.

Contacts	Frequency	Mail	Phone	Field
1. New Product Announcements	4	P	A	S
2. Product Application Information	4	P	A	A
3. Product Updates/New Releases	4	A/S	P	A
4. Case Studies	4	P	S	
a. Product Application				
b. Results				
5. Industry Research	1	S	A/S	P
6. Article Reprints	6	P		
7. Program Specials	12	P	A	A
8. Industry Trends	2	P		
9. Product Uses/Performance Assessment	4		A	P

P = Preferred Medium   A = Acceptable Medium   S = Support Preferred

Figure 4-4 Value-Based Contact Model

© Hunter Business Direct, Inc.

In this model, each type of contact content is matched with frequency and type of media. This gives you the ability to develop specific communication programs with a value-added foundation. For example, this target segment of customers looks for four new product announcements during the year and prefers mail, although phone is acceptable.

The ideal situation would be to ask all customers these same questions in a workshop. This usually isn't economically justified unless significant changes from current practice warrant it. One solution is to conduct workshops around customer segments. For example, if you identified 17 segments in the healthcare market, you would conduct a workshop for each.

Another solution is to ask customers the same type of questions during regular contacts with them. For example, during a phone call, the telemarketing representative could be guided to ask key questions, such as how do they prefer to get new product information. Over time, you could build this type of model for each and every customer.

For example, a 35-year-old company found that, for 7 of the top 10 types of information customers preferred, fax, mail, and phone were acceptable. A shift in contact media meant millions of dollars in savings for the company. Such opportunities require confirmation of customer preferences, careful planning, and trusted leadership.

The contact model gives you a menu of choices for each customer. You have the preferred contact medium, the frequency of contact, and the type of information desired. From this you can build a value-based communication plan for individual customers.

DEVELOPING THE COMMUNICATION/CONTACT PLAN

The next step is to develop a communication/contact plan (shown in Figure 4-7) using the value-based contact model (Figure 4-4) and the external service value analysis. This information is used to build a synchronized marketing and sales program that delivers high value to the customer, builds on the relationship, uses field sales in the most effective manner, and generates increased profits, while minimizing contact costs.

The underlying rationale is to use low-cost contact media to leverage the cost of higher cost contacts. In addition, you base this on an economic model that takes into account the relative value of individual customers.

A comment needs to be made on "response rates." Too often, management has the tendency to focus on measuring response rates on mail and phone. While this may be a valid visible measurement and appear to be helpful as an accountability management tool, it is most often destructive. Rather, management must view this as part of an effort to *leverage* face-to-face contact. In this case, response rates of the media are not relevant.

Economically Grading Customers

Not all customers are equal. Some customers have more potential than others, so you have to develop a method that enables you to recognize these differences in the contact plan. To do that you grade customers in each target segment based on economic considerations. The goal is to increase the number of value-based contacts with the customer, while reducing the overall contact costs. You want the same outcome as was shown earlier in the Team TBA example.

The first step is to recognize you need to match sales expense to expected revenue. Establishing a base sales expense-to-revenue ratio provides a guideline for allocating and leveraging resources. For example, you may determine 15 percent of expected revenue should be allocated for marketing and sales expense. This is then used in developing the communication/contact plan. However, keep in mind, the sales expense-to-revenue ratio for new customer acquisition will be significantly higher.

While expected revenue is one method used for grading customers, it is not the only one. Other valuation types can be used. For example, probably the most effective measurement would be expected lifetime value of each customer. While sales revenue often deals with past events, expected lifetime value takes into account a customer's potential and the ability to achieve that potential.

Several methods can be used to grade customers that go beyond the 80/20 ratio (based on the belief that 20 percent of customers account for 80 percent of revenues) most companies use to rate or grade their accounts. One method, based on account history, assigns customers into A/B/C grades. However, 80/20 or A/B/C types of grading do not allow enough categories to balance frequency of contact media within each grade so that the resources spent best match expected revenue or value.

A better approach is to establish five levels of customer grades, which you would classify as AA, A, B, C, and D. However, don't just base the grades on past purchasing histories.

For example, an account that qualifies as C-level grade may have attributes that mirror A-level accounts. Therefore you may want to reclassify it and see if, with additional attention and resources, its revenues will increase to an A-level account.

Leverage Contact Costs

You want to satisfy the customer's contact preference, but in a way that leverages the effectiveness of higher-cost contact media and balances expenses to expected revenues. Therefore, the first step is to recognize that a *quantum* cost difference exists between contact media, as shown in Figure 4-5.

Each of these contact media has a role in the process and its own level of effectiveness and cost efficiency. The goal is to develop a contact plan that synchronizes communication with the customer in the most effective manner.

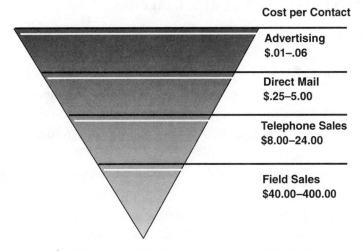

Figure 4-5 Comparative Costs of Contact Media

© Hunter Business Direct, Inc.

ADVERTISING MEDIA AS A CONTACT MEDIUM

Advertising, while being the lowest-cost contact medium, has limited economic value for reaching existing customers. Unless some compelling corporate reason exists, such as brand equity or channel awareness/positioning, advertising is most often used for customer acquisition purposes, i.e., lead generation. Recent studies show companies are shifting their promotional dollars away from media advertising into other forms of marketing, including sales promotion, public relations, direct mail, database-driven loyalty programs, catalog marketing, special events, sponsorships, trade promotions, and so forth. *Advertising Age* estimates 65 percent of all marketing expenditures in the United States now go to these nonmedia sectors.[3]

DIRECT MAIL AS A CONTACT MEDIUM

Too often direct mail is only seen as a means of generating leads for new business, yet it is powerful if used as part of an integrated marketing program. It can be the most efficient (least costly) method of targeting individual customers. It's an ideal medium for delivering information that would be time consuming and nonproductive for a salesperson to deliver.

The classic direct mail package includes a printed piece (brochure, newsletter, catalog, etc.), a cover letter, the envelope, and a response vehicle, typically a bounce-back reply card and an 800 number. Since the size of most business-to-business market segments is relatively small, technology can be used to effectively personalize and individualize the message. A customized letter enables you to repackage the printed piece to meet the external service values of the target customer.

For example, you may have a quarterly newsletter or a new product catalog for mailing. The newsletter contains a variety of items, all relating previously identified external service values. Or, the brochure may be feature-specific and benefit-oriented, containing complete information on the product. In either case, an individual customer is not going to be interested in all the information. Their interest level is going to correspond to their needs.

Segmenting customers based on external service values enables you to customize a cover letter calling attention to those items relating to the customer's specific service values. This approach not only delivers content value (calling attention to the items they are interested in), but also the personalized nature of the correspondence adds value to the relationship. The customer perceives this as being treated as an individual, not as an anonymous account.

Many times when someone sees the contact matrix (Figure 4-7), they state they cannot conceive direct mailing 30 to 40 pieces per year, and certainly not 75 pieces. They do not believe they have enough material to generate that number of mailings. But, when you analyze the number of potential types of information that deliver value to the customer (as defined by the customer), you will find it is not difficult to support at least two mailings per month, and most often, four, five, or six mailings are possible.

For example, a few types of printed pieces that can be mailed to your customers include:

- *Annual report.* With publicly traded companies, at least four opportunities arise to mail something—the annual report and at least three quarterly reports.

- *Application-specific newsletter.* Can be a simple four-page newsletter highlighting product uses and including industry information. This could be produced at least four times per year.

- *Technical bulletin.* Most companies produce product technical specifications or some other type of product information. Developing and mailing four a year is not unreasonable.

- *New product announcement.* A new product announcement can be a new product or a product enhancement. Four a year is not an unreasonable number.

- *Customer satisfaction surveys.* Send copies of results to customers to let them know you are paying attention. Typically, you can do at least two of these per year.

- *Product catalog.* Many companies produce a comprehensive product line catalog in addition to specific information on individual products. Typically, you may have one new catalog each year.

- *Trade shows.* Announcements inviting customers to attend trade shows at which you are exhibiting is a value-based communication. Most companies exhibit in at least two shows per year.

- *Article reprints.* Any articles appearing in industry publications that feature your product should be reprinted and used as a direct mail piece.

- *Press clippings.* On a periodic basis, you should accumulate press clippings about your company and turn them into a mailing piece. This should be done at least twice a year.

As is apparent, it is not difficult to generate twice-a-month mailings. So, as you are building your contact matrix, keep in mind the many opportunities for developing direct mailings.

Advantages of Direct Mail

Direct mail is effective for several reasons.

Pinpoint selectivity. Through personalizing the message, you can target mailings to specific market segments. In some cases, where the market universe is relatively small, you can actually achieve market segments of one, which even allows you to tailor messages to two different people within the same organization.

Videojet, a division of A. B. Dick Inc., is a case in point. The company sells imprinting equipment and found buying decisions were shifting from an individual buyer to committees. A problem resulted from this shift. The individual buyer had been knowledgeable about the equipment and the process and understood that using Videojet-supplied ink was necessary to insure the equipment's productivity. In the long term, this made the Videojet equipment the most cost-effective in the market.

However, the shift to committees involved less knowledgeable individuals interested in saving money, as much as several thousand dollars a year, by buying inferior ink. This would create equipment problems, which Videojet would have to solve. Given this situation, Videojet developed a direct mail campaign to educate the committee members. According to an article in *Business Marketing*, "The company found a well-targeted direct mail campaign to those decision-makers delivered the most impact."[4]

Virtually unlimited format. Direct mail has flexibility in format. It can be a simple printed piece or an elaborate, die-cut fold-out. Any type of format can be used. And, it does not necessarily have to be a printed form. Companies have had success sending videotapes to demonstrate products, using computer diskettes to carry technical information, and using CD-ROMs for elaborate graphical information.

Personal character. Through the cover letter, the direct mail piece is directed to the individual recipient, giving it a personal touch. Address direct mail to individuals, not to job titles or functions.

Unique involvement capability. Direct mail involves the reader. With a customized cover letter pointing to specific information of interest to the recipient, the recipient becomes involved in locating that information and is exposed to other information in the mailing piece.

Timeliness. Direct mail is a timely medium. It has a short turnaround time when compared with advertising and press releases.

No competition. When someone is reading a letter and direct mail piece, they are involved. Whereas, someone on the phone may be performing some action other than totally concentrating on the conversation.

Most testable medium. Direct mail is easy to measure since you provide a feedback mechanism with the direct mail package, bounce-back reply cards with 800 numbers, making it simple to track responses. It also gives you a low-cost means to test various formats and offers.

Low waste. Unlike advertising, you have less wasted circulation.

Low cost. This is often the only economical choice when working with limited budgets and marginal potential return from customers.

Some believe fax is a more effective communication medium and should replace direct mail. Fax has limitations, especially a fixed format. However, fax can be used in select instances. Keep in mind, when sending a fax to a customer, it ties up the customer's equipment and uses their paper. Only use fax when the customer has requested it. That is, use it as part of a contact plan where the customer indicated a preference for fax as the contact medium.

TELEMARKETING AS A CONTACT MEDIUM

Business-to-business telemarketing can be an exceptionally valuable tool. Except for face-to-face contact, it is the only medium that links buyers and sellers in a personal dialogue conducted in real time. Since it is much less expensive than face-to-face contact, it enables a company to have more contact with the marketplace and allows the marketplace to have more contact with the company. The phone allows you to ask questions first and adapt your message to fit the customer's responses.

Telemarketing's flexibility is its strong point. It can be used to supplement face-to-face contact in a synchronized contact program, to generate sales in direct selling, to qualify leads, to serve as the primary contact point for the customer in the Customer Community Center, and to strengthen the effectiveness of other contact media.

For example, when direct mail and telemarketing are combined, the effect is synergistic. Codex Express, the direct marketing operation for Motorola Codex, demonstrated this synergy. The company, which manufactures data communications and networking products, recently ran a test that compared a direct mail only campaign against a mail/telemarketing integrated program. The direct mail only campaign delivered between 1.5 percent and 2 percent conversion to sales. The mail/telemarketing campaign had a 16 percent conversion to sales ratio.[5]

Key Telemarketing Advantages

Telemarketing offers the marketer distinct advantages. Among these are:

- It helps build relationships through one-to-one dialogue.

- It is a bargain when compared to the cost of a sales call.

- It works. When used correctly, the telephone will often generate two-and-one-half to seven times the response achieved by mail alone.

- It is increasingly being used to obtain a competitive advantage through acquisition and management of competitive information.

- It is an excellent method for accumulating customer information essential for relationship building. During each telemarketing contact, customer information is acquired and stored in the database.

- It is adaptable—able to address multiple decision makers. In business-to-business marketing, seldom does one person have decision-making responsibilities. Telemarketing enables the user to maintain personalized contact with all levels of the decision-making process.

- It is synergistic. When used in integrated programs with direct mail and face-to-face contact, it provides powerful support and significantly increases effectiveness.

FACE-TO-FACE AS A CONTACT MEDIUM

Face-to-face is the most expensive and limited form of contact a company has. Yet, face-to-face is the most valuable form of contact since it involves direct, personal interaction with the customer, and most often has the greatest dollars budgeted. This is why it is important to leverage face-to-face with other contact media. Using it as part of an integrated program with phone and mail increases a sales call's productivity, while decreasing overall selling costs.

Why is leveraging so important? Consider the following: Ask your field salespeople to identify how many face-to-face contacts they make in a year with your best customers. Then ask the same for each customer in the next best group, etc. Now add up the contacts. Typically, the sum is two or three times more contacts than the entire salesforce can make. The truth is often salespeople respond with the number of calls they would like to make but just don't have the time. The best customers consume all their time. Leveraging allows adding phone and mail contacts to a customer grade to help free current call volumes for lower value contacts.

To take this a step further, with 180 days of selling in a year, a typical salesperson should be able to sustain three face-to-face contacts per day; that's 540 customer contacts per year per salesperson. Next, multiply this by the number of salespersons and then divide the answer by the number of customers. Then, look at how many times the customer wants to be contacted, average that among all customers, and you will find a wide gap exists between customer expectations and your available resources (field sales). This puts at least some of these customers at risk since they're not getting what they expect.

It is also interesting to look at the perceived coverage field sales representatives offer the AA, A, and B accounts and then look to see if any contact time is left for C and D accounts. One way to fill the gap is to hire more salespeople. A more efficient and effective way is to use low-cost contact media (mail and phone) to increase contact frequency and leverage the field contacts.

Using low-cost contact media satisfies the customer's expectation of contact frequency and more closely matches their optimal value-based contact model, while maximizing the salesperson's effectiveness. At the customer level, perceived service goes up with frequency of value-based contacts, independent of the contact medium. As long as the contact frequency increases and it is value-based, the customer will perceive service as going up and often will not recall the contact medium. Remember, customers' needs center around the quality of the information, not the medium.

DEVELOPING AN INTEGRATED CONTACT PROGRAM

From the information derived through the contact analysis, the value-based contact workshop, and the contact model, a balanced, integrated contact program can be developed.

A contact program must first be economically responsible, i.e., the cost of the planned mix and frequency of contact for a particular customer must match the budgeted expense-to-revenue ratio. So, the first step is to develop an expense-to-revenue ratio for each customer, or customer grade. Each grade in each segment of each target market has an optimal mix of mail, phone, and field contacts for cultivating a relationship within that customer grade level. It could be a 10-4-1 plan, which was one of the earliest published integrated marketing models. NCR used this type of plan to sell cash registers to decentralized purchasing decision makers.

A typical 10-4-1 model is shown in Figure 4-6.

With this, one field contact is supported by fourteen other contacts. This is leveraging the field contact so, when the field salesperson walks into the customer's office, he or she does not have to review all the information passed on to the customer during the fourteen contacts. Rather, the sales representative and customer can focus on those specific concerns the most recent phone contact uncovered.

Customer Contact Matrix

The contact plan uses each of the contact media in the most effective way, keeping in mind the frequency of contact, the customer's preferred method of contact, and the overall cost of customer contact. The model used to develop this is the Customer Contact Matrix (Figure 4-7).

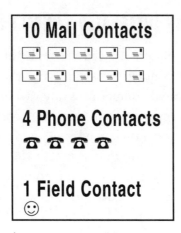

Figure 4-6 10-4-1 Integrated Contact Model

The Customer Contact Matrix provides a detailed contact plan integrating mail, phone, and field sales into an optimal mix. This is an economic model as it balances or reconciles customer contact preferences with the cost to support those contacts.

The model shown in Figure 4-7 covers a one-year program. However, a contact plan can be constructed for any period of time. The steps involved in building a contact matrix are discussed below.

Customer grading. Grading of customers is based on economic attributes. In Figure 4-7, a customer base of 1,000 buyer groups has been segregated into five levels. The criterion for grading used in this model is anticipated sales revenues.

The first two columns of the matrix show the sales category and the number of buyer groups in each grade. For example, the individuals in Category A are expected to generate between $40,000 and $60,000 of sales revenue in the next year, with 150 buyer groups in this category.

Grade/Sales ($000)	1,000=Buyer Groups	CONTACT MEDIA			Sales Cost ($000)	% of Sales Revenues
		Mail ($5)	Phone ($20)	Field ($400)		
		Count	Count	Count		
AA $60+	50	75	50	20	$ 469	13.4%
		3,750	2,500	1,000		
A $40–$60	150	75	40	15	$1,076	14.4%
		11,250	6,000	2,250		
B $20–$40	250	50	25	8	$ 988	13.2%
		12,500	6,250	2,000		
C $10–$20	250	25	12	4	$ 491	13.1%
		6,250	3,000	1,000		
D < $10	300	25	10	1	$ 218	14.5%
		7,500	3,000	300		
Total	1,000	41,250	20,750	6,550	$3,242	13.6%

Figure 4-7 Customer Contact Matrix (Annual)

© Hunter Business Direct, Inc.

When grading, start by rank-ordering buyer groups. Take out the largest accounts (house accounts, national accounts, etc.) as they typically have special integrated plans. Also, take out the small, infrequent buyers when proactive cultivation will not have an economic return. Then take the remaining active buyer groups and divide them into five grades based on the number of buyer groups within each grade. For example, the ratio may look like: AA=the top 5% of active customers; A=15%; B=25%; C=25%; and D=30%.

Determining contact media mix. The next three columns show the contact media. The mail category shows how many individual mailings will be sent to each buyer group along with the total number of mailings for each grade of customer. The phone category shows how many outbound telemarketing contacts will take place during the year and the total number of contacts for that grade of customer. And the field category shows how many field sales calls will take place and the total number of sales per grade.

In the example shown in Figure 4-7, Grade A buyer groups will receive 75 mailings, 40 phone contacts, and 15 face-to-face contacts. Totally, this grade will receive 11,250 mailing pieces, 6,000 phone contacts, and 2,250 face-to-face contacts.

Each grade of buyer group also has a projected cost figure based on the cost of each medium and the contact frequency. For example, in the model, the contact plan for Category A buyer groups is projected to cost $1,076,000, which represents 14.4 percent of total sales revenues expected from this group of buyers ($7.5 million in sales revenues = 150 buyer groups at $50,000 each).

Building a Contact Matrix

The challenge here is to develop a mix of contacts that accomplishes several objectives. First, it must be consistent with the customer's preferences. So, for each tier or grade of customers, you start with the contact preference grid you developed showing the type of contact medium the customer prefers for each contact type (Figure 4-4). The second objective is it must leverage the higher-cost contact media, i.e., wherever practical, use the lower-cost contact medium more frequently. The final objective is to stay within the budget for this grade.

One way to meet these objectives is to start with face-to-face contacts. Take the face-to-face contacts customers have listed as being preferable. Typically, this exceeds what the budget allows. So, move some of the field sales contact content into telemarketing and direct mail until reaching a balance between sales costs and contact preferences.

You may have to modify the mix several times, keeping in mind the cost constraints and the goal of leveraging higher-cost contact media to hit the targeted cost of sales. Remember: *contact frequency is usually more important than contact medium.*

Another factor to consider is the effectiveness of the contact. For example, a Category A customer will receive three times the mailings as a Category C customer. Therefore, mailings to a Category C customer must deliver, on average, three pieces of information, which means the communication to the customer is less focused and less current.

Figure 4-8 shows a summary of the contacts in the matrix. Based on the contact matrix (Figure 4-7), this sample has 41,250 mailing pieces, 20,750 phone contacts, and 6,550 field sales contacts for all categories of customers.

		Mail	Phone	Field	% of Sales
Total Contacts	78,550	41,250	20,750	6,550	
Average Cost of each	$47.28	$5.00	$20.00	$400.00	
Total Cost ($000)	$3,241	$206	$415	$2,620	13.6

Figure 4-8 Contact Matrix Summary

© Hunter Business Direct, Inc.

This type of summary enables you to better plan and budget for an integrated marketing program. As an example, an outbound telemarketing representative typically makes 25 contacts per day or 6,250 contacts per year. Therefore, 20,750 contacts require 3.5 telemarketing representatives.

When the Customer Contact Matrix is complete, the next step is to create a monthly planning calendar. First define the potential contacts and the contact frequency. Then build a plan, for example, for A-level accounts. This should contain all contacts, the month and date on which each will happen, and which type of contact is included in that communication. Next, you develop a weekly contact plan for A-level accounts, showing which contacts (media) are going to be included in each week's communication. Figure 4-9 shows a typical weekly plan for A-grade customers in a segment.

Date	Medium	Contact Content
9/1	Mail	New product announcement — TechWiz
9/1–9	Phone	Highlight of upcoming trade show
9/5	Mail	Case history on Application #7
9/10–18	Phone	Follow up on TechWiz mailing reviewing benefits and applications

Figure 4-9 Weekly Contacts for Customers

The Customer Contact Matrix simply builds on what companies are already doing. A typical marketing operation does much of this planning already, especially on what types of communication are going to be used during a predetermined period of time. Where this differs significantly from the traditional approach to marketing and sales is: *Plan your selling and communications first around what the* customer *wants you to do, rather than around what* you *want to do.* Another key difference is that the contact frequency for the customer is predefined and communications must fit into the plan.

This customer-focused approach to communications optimizes the sales and marketing expenditures necessary for delivering value to customers. It determines the optimal mix of contact media to support different levels of existing customers.

CREATING VALUE-BASED COMMUNICATION

The message, or content, and the medium for customer communications evolves naturally through this process. External service values provide the product attributes that impact purchasing behavior. The customer's contact preferences arise from the workshop and other techniques. Using the Customer Contact Matrix, you can develop specific communication programs around marketing objectives.

To illustrate this, consider the case of a business furniture manufacturer who has developed a new line of semi-enclosed workstations featuring environmental controls. The new workstations were a result of identifying unfulfilled needs of current customers. A segment of customers, software programmers, had indicated they would like to be able to individually adjust the heating or cooling in cubicles since their work hours often ran late into the night. A white-noise generator was also included in the new workstation to minimize background distractions.

The marketing objective is to get 20 percent of current customers in the target segment to upgrade to this new-style workstation. The first step is to identify the target segment, which are those buyer groups in the customer database involved with programming applications.

When the target segment is generated, the next step involves further segmentation into clusters having similar external service values. This produces the target audiences for communication.

With the target market segments determined, the next step involves identifying the contact medium to be used for individual customers. In this instance, assume all customers indicated they preferred mail for new product information.

At this point, the communication contact plan is reviewed to schedule mailings related to the new product. Two mailings will be sent to AA, A, and B grade customers, and one mailing to C and D grades.

The first mailing will include product literature, a personalized cover letter, a mailing envelope, a response card, and an 800 number. The product literature's content will emphasize the new features and include key benefits previously identified as external service values. The personalized letter will call attention to the new features and reemphasize those specific external service values important to that customer. This same package would be sent to all customer grades.

The second mailing, sent three weeks later, goes only to those who did not respond to the first mailing in the AA, A, and B grades. The literature remains the same, but the personalized letter reminds the customer about the new product.

Also, it asks the customer, in the event the new product is not of interest, to forward the information to someone else in the organization who may have an interest. Both mailings must fit the mail schedule.

After the second mailing is sent, the product announcement is added to the next telemarketing phone call list of topics. For those customers who do not respond, it's a reminder. For those who did respond, it's a thank-you and follow-up. And, the field salesperson has access to the same information for his or her next customer sales call.

Through this process, the communication content has been predetermined through the external service values. The medium used to deliver the information has been defined by the customer. And, by integrating mail, phone, and face-to-face contacts, the customer receives information of value to them, which significantly increases the likelihood of purchases. In addition, the product introduction is aimed at a pre-qualified target market, which makes for more cost efficient marketing and sales.

COMMUNITY BUILDING IN ACTION: BUSINESSFORMS

In building an integrated contact plan, the first step the BusinessForms division took was to analyze each customer contact point, including catalog mailings, forms quotes, invoices, new product information, and phone contacts. Next, telemarketers and field sales representatives asked each customer which contact medium they preferred for each type of information.

The results showed that most dentists preferred receiving new product information through the mail with a phone follow-up, yet preferred face-to-face contact when receiving a new forms quote.

After the BusinessForms division conducted the contact and media preference analyses, they conducted a value-based contact workshop with a group of dentists who represented different practice types, from large group practices to solo practices. The workshop, while focusing on contact preferences and content, also further refined the external service values.

The workshop conversations revealed that the forms dentists used included computer-generated forms, such as building business aids, patient billing forms, insurance provider billing forms, and government billing forms.

Another part of the workshop focused on the distribution system preferred by the dentist, which impacted the contact media. It found a basic division: in practices where the dentists were part of a large *medical* practice, buying was done face-to-face. In *dental* practices, mail and phone were preferred. This information led to building a contact preference model for the dental segment through a single channel.

The next step involved economically grading customers. This significantly altered the way in which customers are communicated with. The first decision was to determine the cut-off point for grading. They determined customers with at least a $400,000 practice would be classified as active customers and would be put into the account management program. Those with less than this amount would be assigned to a separate category, one that would be reactive rather than proactive. Customers in this category would receive a forms catalog four times a year and would be supported with inbound customer service.

Next, the division graded its active customers into five categories—AA/A/B/C/D—and an account management contact plan was developed for each customer grade similar to the one shown in Figure 4-7.

With this step completed, the BusinessForms division developed value-based communications that supported the contact plan. For example, since this same process was followed for all segments of the healthcare market, they were able to identify common forms used in all segments. From this, they developed a catalog containing these common sets of forms, and then added product information specific to dentists.

When the catalog was mailed, a personalized cover letter was used to call attention to products specifically designed to meet the individual dentist's needs and to focus on the specific dentist's style of practice. For example, some dentists use humorous reminders in reactivating patients to schedule a routine cleaning and examination. Products that fit this description were noted in the cover letter.

The dentist not only received product information, but value was added by recognizing the individual dentist's needs. This built a customer community—making each contact with the customer deliver value, as defined by the customer, which leads to a greater interdependence between the customer and the supplier.

Notes

1. William H. Davidow and Bro Uttal, *Total Customer Service: The Ultimate Weapon* (New York: Harper & Row, 1989), 32.

2. Regis McKenna, *Relationship Marketing: Successful Strategies for the Age of the Customer* (Reading, Mass: Addison-Wesley, 1991), 112.

3. Stan Rapp and Thomas L. Collins, *Beyond MaxiMarketing: The New Power of Caring and Daring* (New York: McGraw-Hill, 1994), 26–28.

4. Sandra Pesmen, "Direct Mail Campaign Helps Videojet Get Back into 'Black Ink'," *Business Marketing*, November 1991, 58–59.

5. Kate Bertrand, "A potent combination," *Business Marketing*, November 1991, 58.

5

THE DATABASE AS A MARKETING TOOL

The database is what makes a customer community possible. It serves *as the memory of all customer transactions and the treasury of values*. It continually provides provisions in the form of recorded needs, comments, purchases, inquiries, and concerns that nourish you on your customer community exploration. It is the foundation for work in segmentation, account management, and targeted new customer acquisition.

The database enables you to engage in a meaningful and valuable dialogue with the customer that leads to the spirit of community. The simplicity, economics, and software availability to build, manage, and use a contact database allows you to return to personal relationship marketing that has, for centuries, described successful sales. People prefer to do business in this new civil environment and will not return to the more abusive and self-serving days of mass marketing.

PROCESS, NOT TECHNOLOGY

Too often companies rush headlong into acquiring hardware and software for a database without considering how they plan to use it. This is the most visible evidence of a contact database and naturally is the focus of most conversation. It's also a tangible expense to be budgeted and capitalized, unlike the cost of training and productivity, which are softer economic measures.

While a database may use technology, first and foremost it's built as a process. Keep in mind the database is for customer information. You need to determine what customer information goes into the database and how you intend to use the information. This has nothing to do with technology. Rather it has everything to do with how you gather and use customer information.

A good example of not being concerned with technology is the Catheterization Lab Calling Program used by Eigen in Nevada City, California. They use 5″ × 8″ notecards to collect information on the 1,300–1,400 catheterization labs they service. The notecards are in shoe boxes and four salespeople work the phones, using the cards and colored paper clips for follow-up. The company has been so successful with their "database" that major companies, like Siemens and GE, come to them to find out how Eigen often can identify new business opportunities first.

TEN KEYS TO DATABASE SUCCESS

Extensive experience in designing and building a database for business-to-business marketers and research conducted for the National Conference of Database Managers (NCDM) led to developing these ten guidelines for a successful marketing database.

1. Database Marketing Is Not a Technology Issue

Successful databases are built to serve the needs of customers and those employees who serve customers. Functional requirements are defined by these needs and they drive the design and operation of the database. Logic demands understanding and documenting, with discipline and completeness, what you want to do with the database. This is the logical first step. Companies who have built successful account/contact management systems say planning, discipline, and integration are the keys, rather than technology.

Another factor is sales representatives and other marketing channel partners need to share contact information. It sometimes requires a cultural change because salespeople believe they "own" customer information. This is especially true of channel partners, such as independent sales organizations and resellers. Unless you have access to the end user, you will be unable to compete successfully, which is a loss to your channel partner.

It should also be noted that technology does not change behaviors. For example, sales automation and a database will not solve basic field reporting issues rooted in the behavior of people and the organization's culture.

2. Chart the Process

Planning and discipline are two major factors in a successful database. Planning defines what the requirements are for the

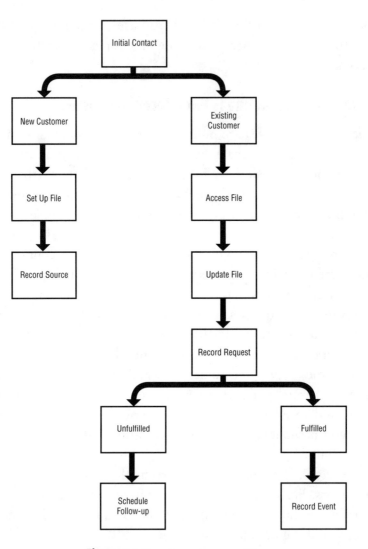

Figure 5-1 Database Process Chart

data and the discipline is that you stick with the plan. In the planning stages, it helps to draw a picture or a process chart of how the database is going to work. This shows how information and documents are transferred and managed. By putting the process down on paper, it becomes easier to see what really happens. The chart should be reviewed with everyone involved. Sales needs to agree to it, as do dealers, telemarketers, and customer service representatives. Having the process charted gives those involved an effective means of validating how they are going to use the data.

To show how this works, consider a basic incoming call from a customer. Figure 5-1 illustrates the process.

In this example, when a call comes in, the first step is determining if the call is from a current customer or a new customer. To chart the steps, you need to talk with the contact "owner," who was identified when you developed the contact log discussed in Chapter 4. For example, in this case, information from a new customer would include the individual's name, functional title and buyer group, organization, and location. Other information may include SIC code, number of employees, annual sales, etc. This would be entered in a new file for the database. As you go through this process, you identify the types of information you need to capture. By charting the process, you give everyone involved an opportunity to validate the information requirements. Then you need to take the next step, which is to see how you would use the information. Here, you may want to plot the reports you plan to use during the next year and then identify the information needed for the reports.

3. Manual First, Then Automate

Just as technology is not the issue, automation is not that important. It is the process that counts. Develop a hard-copy database first. Use notecards or some other paper-based system. This has several advantages:

- Physical documents are easier to learn.

- Physical documents have "real" value to the user.

- Management has something tangible to touch.

- For many, technology is a "black hole" and physical documents give people reassurance the process will work.

4. Be Rigid, Not Flexible

Establish the limitations of the database and be firm. More flexibility and more data is not better. The major downfall is the lack of use, lack of confidence, and poor data quality. If you offer too many options, people will have a difficult time determining which are important. Limit the scope of the initial database and stay firm. Manage expectations!

5. Build a Prototype, Not a Pilot

If you start with a pilot program, it too often takes on a life of its own and is difficult to get approval from everyone who wants, or thinks they need, to be involved. With a prototype, you are announcing this is not permanent. This may sound like semantics. But, a prototype has a short-term measurable business value and, many times, is viewed as a learning experience. It has less political baggage. Keep the planning stages of the database flexible so you can make wholesale changes if necessary.

6. Use a Simple, But Proven, Software Package

A number of commercially available software packages are available. These include Act, Telemagic, Goldmine, Onyx, Incontext, Vantive, Brock, and Win Sales, to name a few. Different levels of software are available for what you want to do. In fact, experience shows that the software functionality typically exceeds what most companies are able to implement. Moreover, recent product upgrades have widened that gap. It's best to use what is available and learn from what others have found to be successful.

By defining your application first, you have a clearer idea of the level of software support needed. When evaluating database software, some guidelines are:

- The software vendor should have at least ten installations similar to yours.

- The salesperson should be a teacher, not a vendor. The salesperson should help teach you how to use the software to your advantage.

- You should have access to other users who have similar installations so you can learn from their successes and failures.

- Clearly outline output reports and selects, where appropriate, so you can match these with the software's functions.

- Keep it simple. Seldom do you need a software program that runs on a mainframe. In fact, if marketing is to retain ownership of the database, then you may want to install it using a client-server computer network.

7. Collect Only Data You Will Use in the Next Twelve Months

Too often, companies building a database want it to contain every possible piece of information they have in their files. Information you put into a database that is not planned to be used in the next twelve months is wasted information. It just takes up disk space and, more importantly, pollutes your database as unused data tends to destroy data credibility. If not used in twelve months, when you do come to use the data, you will most likely find it is woefully out-of-date and needs to be changed.

In a recent study, 95 percent of the companies sampled had less than five database applications running. Limit applications to those actually being used.

Also, when entering customer information, use functional titles as well as business titles for individuals. The reason for this is most commercial databases have overlays based on functional titles.

8. Centralize Data Entry and Validate Outside Input

The experience of many database users is salespeople are the wrong people to maintain the database. Unless a "one-finger, two-touch" method is used for entering information, a salesperson won't bother. The result is they won't enter all information or they will enter incomplete information that pollutes the database. Basically, they are not interested in, or behaviorally suited for, following a set of procedures necessary to maintain data integrity, such as keying standards for name and address. This type of activity does not match their personality characteristics and they do not consider it their primary role.

The most effective approach is to have telemarketers in the Customer Community Center take the responsibility of maintaining the database. However, controls are needed, including:

- Mandate data entry standards.

- Audit data integrity (input and consolidation).

- Outsource all external file overlays.

A technique that works effectively is to have salespeople call into a voice mail system following a customer meeting and provide details from that meeting. This then is accessed by the data entry operator to update the database. Xerox ran a study on having direct field sales input data or use voice mail input. Voice mail won hands down as it preserved the accuracy of data and required less time on the salesperson's part.

9. Build and Refresh Database On-Line with Telemarketing

The Customer Community Center is the centralized location used for building and refreshing the database. Here, all telemarketing, lead management, order processing, and customer service functions are implemented. These are key aspects of the database. Therefore, locate the functions of the database within this group. Use those functions that have high contact frequency on-line to access and update the information, which translates to high data integrity.

10. Focus on Any Output Used Outside Your Control

Manage expectations by focusing on output outside your direct control. If your contact database provides information used outside your direct control, you need to educate, regularly monitor, and get feedback from these people. Otherwise, their expectations may be beyond the ability of the database to deliver.

This is a dynamic process, you need feedback from users on how you can improve. These basic operating principles will help:

- Understanding is key to use. It adds to value.

- Value must be obvious, tangible, short term, and monetary.

- Customer retention equals profits.

- Acceptance must be enthusiastic (champion your cause).

BUILDING A DATABASE

In building a database, four key issues must be considered—individual orientation, segmentation, cultivation, and database ownership.

Individual-Oriented Structure

First, all transaction information must be linked to the individual. The basic premise underlying the database, and the customer community, is that relationships are built and offers (products/services) made to the individual—not the account or organization—for a specific business application. Five levels of information are mandatory:

1. *Individual name:* the actual name of the customer contact.

2. *Buyer group:* the functional title or the application group represented by this buyer.

3. *Location:* the street address of the individual.

4. *Corporate identifier:* the corporate or division name associated with the individual.

5. *Affiliates:* other divisions or affiliates of the parent organization.

All transaction information—phone contact logs, quotes, contracts, purchase orders, shipments, invoices, and so on—must be linked to the individual to maintain a comprehensive transaction history. Other attributes, such as SIC code, number of employees, annual sales, etc., can be attached to the level most appropriate within the database and used as selects in database searches. For example, SIC code may be attached to the location level or at the corporate level.

The economic value of the customer is defined by his or her relation to the buyer group. The individuals in a buyer group are the corporate stewards and trustees responsible for a business application and it is the matching of the business application with your product/service that creates the economic foundation for the relationship.

Segmenting Individuals

With this individual data, including transaction and attribute information, you can then begin to cluster or segment individuals into meaningful groups. If you recognize individuals have specific needs and ways of doing business, it is then reasonable to cluster individuals with common needs and purchasing behaviors for your business application. This is target marketing.

This should not be a complicated process. Experience shows, within any single target or segment, customers buy based on a limited number of reasons. Typically, 80 percent of purchasing behavior can be attributed to fewer than seven external service values.

Customer Cultivation

The database is an important tool for implementing the customer contact plan described in Chapter 4. The first function of the contact plan and database is to preserve existing business at the individual and product line levels. The next function is one of cultivation, growing your business through expanding your product offerings to individual customers and then expanding your penetration to reach every significant person within the buyer's location that could have an application for your products or services. Chapter 7 provides a detailed discussion of the cultivation process.

Database Ownership

Marketing and sales must own (have economic budgeting authority and responsibility) for the contact database, not MIS. You need to establish this at the earliest stages of planning.

This is a very real issue. Too often, companies automatically turn to MIS for database solutions. However, as Lisa Petrison and Paul Wang of Northwestern University found in interviews with marketing and MIS managers, conflicts of interest can be severe. Issues that arise include costs and system utilization. MIS has as their priority reduced costs, while marketing wants a system up and running quickly. Also, MIS expects a marketing database to be static, like an accounting database, whereas a marketing database needs to be flexible and continually requires modifications or changes.[1]

These conflicts need resolution and the database works best under the control of marketing and sales. Keep in mind, MIS, while technically knowledgeable about databases, does not typically understand the underlying basis for the marketing database and certainly is not going to drive the new application of information in servicing the customer. They are often more comfortable working with more tangible data structures, such as found in manufacturing and finance. Here, the requirements are often internally defined, better documented, and more easily and visibly monitored.

USING THE DATABASE

The database plays an important role in virtually all aspects of marketing and sales. Following is an overview of these areas, which include: research, planning, field sales support, dealer support, stand-alone sales, productivity improvement, new customer acquisition, new customer assimilation, customer reactivation, and customer cultivation.

Research

The database is ideally suited for storing both external customer research and internal operational customer research. The more you know about the individual customer, such as the decision-making process, buying cycles, applications of interest, unfulfilled needs, etc., the more directed your marketing activities can become. Typical research activities include:

- *Customer satisfaction*

- *Employee satisfaction*

- *Needs assessment*

- *Attribute profiles*

- *Targeting segments*

An example of using the database for research is Excelan, a marketer of circuit boards and software in San Jose, California, who identified a shift in customers' buying behavior from a technical product focus to an office automation orientation. This discovery influenced the marketing and sales managers' decisions about hiring and training employees as well as about selecting and developing new target markets.[2] Research provides feedback and customer feedback is foundational to community building.

Planning

The information in the database provides a powerful planning tool. It makes available significant information on all aspects of the customer relationship. Applications include:

- *Strategic insights*

- *Product input*

- *Account grading*

- *Contact plans*

- *Sales expense-to-revenue analysis*

For example, in the early days of Hewlett-Packard's Customer Information Center, management quickly realized they had a direct contact with the customer and actively used that for product design.

Leverage and Support Field Sales

The database helps leverage high-cost contact medium, such as field sales, and supports field sales efforts through telemarketing and mail activities. Ways to use the database include:

- *Qualify leads*

- *Introduce new reps*

- *New rep accountability*

- *Make appointments*

- *Handle customer service and billing problems*

- *Follow up on rep calls*

- *Advance the sales process*

According to Tom Scott, vice president of sales at Toshiba, "Telesales is a seamless extension of our field sales." The database can support mailings, faxes, and phone contacts in an integrated, synchronized, interdependent process with the field. This interdependency in the sales community is the nucleus of the customer community.

Leverage and Support Dealer Channels

Just as the database can be used to leverage and support the sales force, it can perform those same types of functions for the dealer channel:

- *Generate and qualify leads*

- *Recruit dealers*

- *Activate and grow dealers*

- *Dealer locator/referral*

- *Pull-through programs*

Both Toshiba and Lexmark are examples of how the database is used to support dealer channels. Toshiba sells its popular laptop computers exclusively through a network of more than 4,500 dealers. An integrated program of fax, mail, and phone, driven by the information in the database, enables Toshiba to maintain close contact with their dealers.

Prior to using an integrated program and the database, Lexmark (which contracts for the IBM typewriter trademark) had 25 field sales representatives trying to service more than 500 typewriter dealers nationally. This meant a very high sales cost per dealer. Today, fewer field sales representatives are used with mail and telemarketing, which results in increased service levels and access for the dealers at a lower cost/dealer ratio.

Stand-Alone Sales Channel

Another database function is to use direct marketing as a stand-alone sales channel. This sales channel handles the entire product line and all sales functions. Functions include:

- *Lead generation and management*

- *Close sales*

- *Sell related products/services*

- *Enter the order*

- *Fulfillment*

- *Customer service*

- *Collection*

Dell Computer falls into this category. Their sales efforts are through advertising, direct mail, and telemarketing, with the database as a key element. As Michael Dell commented: "Of course, we use it [the database] for direct mail. But what it mostly does for us is provide a familiarity with the customer—a comfort level that personalizes the relationship.

Customers who call are not just dealing with Dell Computer Corporation, they are dealing with people they are used to dealing with and who know about them and what happened when they called before."[3]

Once a customer is entered into Dell's database, every call a customer places gets preferential treatment. Accessing the database, the Dell phone representative can display the customer's complete transaction and company history—who they are, what they do, when they first inquired, when they bought, what they bought, their previous thoughts on system configuration, their technical concerns, etc. The representative sees, at a glance, what equipment they have, what their repair history has been, and can make sure what they are ordering will be appropriate to their needs and will work well with what they already have.[4]

Another company that uses the database for order processing is Quill Corporation, a $200 million mail-order office supply company. In surveying customers, the company found nearly 25 percent had computers with modems. So, the company developed a system taking advantage of modems that speeds the order processing time and saves customers money in long-distance time.

Customers can connect via computer and modem with Quill's order processing system and use their own computers to key in their orders. The system walks the customer through easy-to-use steps. It automatically tracks each customer's new order, and it can assist the buyer by generating a list that includes previous orders, and by creating a "reminder list" to assist in the product ordering. It even provides a "memo" capability to allow the customer to contact Quill electronically using an e-mail system.[5]

Improve Productivity

The database contributes to improved productivity at all levels of the marketing and sales operation. It's used for:

- *Leveraging*

- *Tracking and measuring results*

- *Evaluating sales and marketing programs*

- *Continuous improvement*

Productivity is a central economic value created by a successful contact database. This productivity is driven by better targeting and managing of relationships so measurements tend to emphasize effectiveness more than efficiency.

Acquire New Customers

Customer acquisition relies on the database for a number of functions. Targeting the right prospects is most important. Knowing an inquirer's potential value and how to best qualify and manage the sale is another valuable role of the database. This requires using a single database for prospects and customers. Chapter 8 looks more closely at the acquisition process and the use of the database. Some of the applications include:

- *Generate leads*

- *Qualify leads*

- *Cultivate prospects*

- *Manage leads*

- *Advance the sales process*

- *Close the loop*

- *Assess and refine lead quality*

Assimilate New Customers

Too often companies ignore the new customer. Once the order has been received, the customer becomes another number on an account list. New customers need to be "assimilated" into the customer community. Building a relationship with the new customer begins with establishing the dimensions of the relationship. This involves:

- *Thanking them*

- *Reinforcing buying decision*

- *Measuring satisfaction*

- *Collecting valuable personal, buyer group, location, and corporate information*

- *Rewarding/stimulating repeat purchases*

- *Resolving problems*

Hour for hour, and dollar for dollar, the most profit and growth is available in assimilation.

Cultivate Customers

The database plays a critical role in the customer cultivation process, described in Chapter 7. Cultivation builds loyalty. It provides emotional nourishment to your employees. And, it is a powerful economic contributor because it acquires new revenues at a relatively low cost and creates more loyal and valuable customers:

- *Product penetration*

- *Buyer group penetration*

- *Location penetration*

- *Service aftermarket needs*

- *Introduce/sell new products/services*

- *Uncover additional/new needs*

- *Nurturing and building loyalty*

For example, Borg Warner Chemical Co., whose customers are custom molders of thermoplastics, developed an on-line database that provides customers up-to-date technical product data about color, grade, strength, weight, and processing conditions; new product announcements; and ordering information. Providing this capability to the customer resulted in an increase in orders for a new plastic application the company never understood it had.[6]

In another case, the database showed a company how it could grow without adding products or customers. This manufacturer of products for the financial community has six major product lines. Their customer research showed the major detriment to further growth was that customers had bought all the products. Yet, the database profile showed the average customer had only purchased 1.6 product lines. With an active cultivation program, the company could double or triple their business without adding products or customers.

Reactivate Former Customers

The database gives access to dormant or former customers. Their names should be maintained in the database with some type of coding that indicates potential for reactivation. Many times, just taking the action of contacting a former customer can rekindle the customer's interest. Some of the activities supported by the database include:

- *Reintroducing the company*

- *Emphasizing the customer s importance*

- *Resolving problems*

- *Identifying unfulfilled needs*

- *Offering an incentive*

To show how this can work, a major oil company used their database to find those customers who had recently stopped using the oil company's fleet credit card. They sent those dormant customers a simple letter reaffirming the value of the fleet card and asking them (with no incentive) to come back as a customer. This resulted in a 15 percent reactivation, which produced a three-week payback on the mailing and resulted in thousands of gallons of added sales. World-class companies are testing cards and more personal communication to further extend these types of programs.

While the database can provide you with a wealth of information, don't be misled by database information; it can be deceptive. Take the case of a traditional men's shoe manufacturer. This company expanded their product line as a means of survival. After a short period of time, they began to notice their customer's shoe sizes were shrinking and adjusted their product offerings accordingly. It wasn't until just before the company went bankrupt that they realized their database reports did not separate men's and women's shoes.

COMMUNITY BUILDING IN ACTION: BUSINESSFORMS

When the BusinessForms division designed their database, they went back to the plans they had developed. They looked at the external service values, the grading of accounts, and the customer contact plan. These provided the guidelines for the type of information needed in the database in addition to the basics of name, location, etc.

The division determined what type of campaigns they would be running and documented each for the next twelve months.

Since they learned dentists differ in the style of their approach with patient reactivation mailings, they needed to know if the dentist uses a humorous approach, classical approach, or contemporary approach. This determined product offerings they made available to the dentist.

Other information about the dentist that was necessary was the software they use, which indicates what type of forms they use for accounting. The company also needed to know how they acquired the dentist. If it were through a software alliance, an accounting firm, or a third party, they needed to keep track of royalties. If it were through a catalog mailing, this enabled them to better measure the effectiveness of their marketing communication programs.

Another data category involved whether the dentist is part of a multiple location group or franchise. With multiple location operations, a major concern is maintaining the integrity and appearance of graphic conventions the group uses. So, the division needed this information in the database since it becomes an external service value for marketing to this segment of dentists.

Another dimension of the database involved relationship building information. For example, the division wanted to keep track of when a dentist started his or her practice so they could send anniversary cards. They wanted to keep track of the birthdays of individuals involved in the order process. And, they needed to know if the individual in the database was a decision maker or the order placer when introducing new products.

These are just some of the categories of information the division put into their database. The key is to use the account management contact plan as the driver for database information. Then, decide what types of information will be used in marketing and sales programs before deciding on what technology to use. The technology and software depends on the type of information in the database and how it will be used.

Notes

1. Lisa A. Petrison and Paul Wang, "Relationship Issues in Creating the Customer Database: The Potential for Interdepartmental Conflict Between Marketing and MIS," *Journal of Direct Marketing* 7:4, Autumn 1993, 58.

2. Rowland T. Moriarty and Gordon S. Swartz, "Automation to Boost Sales and Marketing," *Harvard Business Review*, January–February 1989, 103.

3. Stan Rapp and Thomas L. Collins, *Beyond MaxiMarketing: The New Power of Caring and Daring* (New York: McGraw-Hill, 1994), 71.

4. Ibid., 74–75.

5. Ronald S. Kauffman, *Future$ell: Automating Your Sales Force* (Boulder, CO: Cross Communications Company, 1990), 92–93.

6. Rene M. Dallaire, "Data-Based Marketing for Competitive Advantage," *Information Strategy*, Spring 1992, 6.

6

CREATING THE CUSTOMER COMMUNITY CENTER

The Customer Community Center (C^3) is the centerpiece for building a community. It brings together the functions necessary for building a spirit of community and leveraging the company's functional skills. It's the centralized information center, collecting information from and disseminating information to the customer. It executes the contact plan and delivers external service values through value-based communication. It is the functional location through which customer contact information is planned and managed.

While the growing trend in business-to-business marketing to consolidate customer contact points into a centralized location was originally driven out of a search for efficiency, consistency, and competency, the C^3 has an even greater economic value: creating customer loyalty.

The C³ operates under a variety of names. In some organizations, it's called the Telecenter, as the telephone is the most visible medium used; in others, it is the Customer Care Center or Customer Service Center. (For example, Toshiba refers to it as "Customer Server.") The term *Customer Community Center* is more appropriate since, through it, you nurture and deepen your relationship with individual customers directly and through your resellers.

Regardless of the name, the one overriding objective of the C³ is to make it easier for the customer to do business with you, which builds customer loyalty and enables you to build profitable, long-term relationships. The following are a list of triggers that indicate potential corporate benefit from a C³:

- have a field sales force

- need to improve sales force productivity

- need to strengthen customer relations

- have the necessary resources to build and sustain a center

- have disjointed sales and marketing activities

- have separate business units that sell or service the same customer

- sell direct to the end customer

- have distributors with exclusive territories and who have a close relationship with the customer.

THE ROLE OF THE C³

The basic objective of the C³ is to make it easier for the customer to do business with you, which builds customer loyalty through improved customer service. This is not the case where, as some managements do, you install an 800 number and then assign some people to answer it. This is a short-sighted approach doomed to failure.

The first step is to minimize the number of people the customer needs to contact—consolidating all contact points into a central source. The customer then has a single location to contact for answers to most of their questions and for tracking content of all customer contacts. Typically, 40 percent of the calls to a C³ are order specific and another 40 percent are product specific. Only between 6 and 8 percent are product inquiries requiring a product specialist. This means a high percentage of all calls can be answered with one contact.

To show the seriousness of this issue, consider the experience of GTE in California. In 1992, as part of an overall reengineering process, the company determined only one customer call out of every 200 had their call or problem resolved positively. Customers often had to speak with as many as seven different people. GTE set up seven Customer Care Centers that have a "two-touch" commitment, which means the customer will never have to talk with more than two employees to resolve a problem.[1]

Another aspect of the C³ is that the telephone enables building a dialogue between the customer and the representative.

Once a dialogue has been established, it is possible to capture information about your customer that will enable you to build profitable relationships and economically develop new customers that look like your best current customers. It enables you to build a comprehensive profile of your customer.

The C^3 delivers the following:

- Increases the productivity of the field sales force or sales channel. Experience shows an immediate 15 percent increase in sales productivity is a reasonable expectation.

- Provides a competitive advantage in the marketplace through improved customer service.

- Allows the sharing of information within and between different business units.

- Provides better control of marketing opportunities.

- Integrates lower-cost direct mail and telemarketing into the selling process.

- Improves accountability of sales and marketing dollars.

A customer community is formed when these strategies and tactics come together to build a sustainable relationship with the customer.

THE END, NOT THE BEGINNING

To build a successful C^3, you must put the customer, not the technology, first. Experience from designing customer centers, prototyping centers, and actually operating centers, shows certain steps must be taken to achieve a successful operation.

These stages can be summarized as gathering background data, modeling the C³, scoping the size of the C³, determining measurements, and creating an implementation plan.

Gathering Background Data

The first step is to gain an understanding of what types of customer contact activities are taking place within the organization, which is what you did when compiling a contact log (Figures 4-2 and 4-3). Now you select which contact types will be handled through the Customer Community Center. Most people tend to include all contacts in the C³. However, while the majority of contacts can be handled through the C³, some contact types, due to their specialized or infrequent nature, are not appropriate. Rather, you should concentrate on the most common types with the highest volumes, where most customer information will be managed. For example, recently a company just wanted to use the center for lead qualification. So, this was the only contact type included in their design of the center.

The communication programs also influence planning. Figure 6-1 reproduces the summary of the customer contact matrix developed in Chapter 4. From this you can see the C³ has to handle 41,250 mailings and 20,750 outbound phone contacts.

	Mail	Phone	Field	% of Sales
Total Contacts	78,550	41,250	20,750	6,550	
Average Cost of Each	$47.28	$5.00	$20.00	$400.00	
Total Cost ($000)	$3,241	$206	$415	$2,620	13.6

Figure 6-1 Contact Matrix Summary

Designing a C³ Model

At this point the physical model of the C³ can be developed. Based on the background data, you can estimate budgets based on actual volume reported and planned from each contact point and the anticipated time requirements to process transactions. This provides you with hard data, not "guesstimates."

You can now begin sizing the center for square footage, staffing, phone equipment, computers, etc. Since you have realistic data gathered from the contact points, this part of the process should be relatively accurate.

Figure 6-2 summarizes the steps in the planning process.

These, in essence, are the steps that must be taken before setting up the customer center. With this process, you are analyzing current customer behaviors and then developing a centralized communication/service operation that supports those behaviors.

In-House or Outsource?

After reviewing the planning process, many organizations face the decision of whether to develop the C³ as an internal project or use an outside source. After becoming aware of the functions inherent in the C³, management may determine they do not have the internal tools, processes, competencies, or culture to plan, develop, and operate a C³.

Pilots, prototypes, and outsourcing. Several options can be considered when setting up a C³. If you determine outside assistance is needed, you can hire an outside consultant who can provide several levels of service including designing

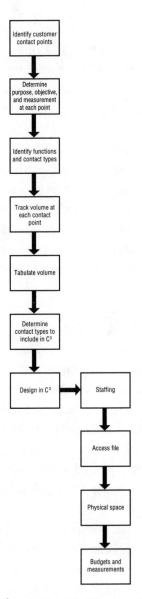

Figure 6-2 C³ Design Planning Process

a center, designing and building a pilot center for testing and evaluation purposes, designing and building a prototype that will eventually be operated by the company, and designing, building, and operating the center for the company. The primary values of outsourcing are: velocity, low start-up cost, and faster learning by your team.

At times, a company wants to consolidate contact points into a center but is unsure or not experienced in direct marketing. A consultant can be used to analyze the objectives and requirements of the center and then design a center based on the processes described above. This would be operated by the company. The consultant may simply prepare the plans for the center with the company responsible for implementing. Or, the consultant may also be involved in staffing, equipment selection, and space design.

Another option is to design and build a pilot program. This typically is used to test and learn how to build the best center. That is, to see how a center fulfills the sales and marketing objectives and if the company has the core competencies to operate a center. For example, a center was designed and built to handle lead qualification. The pilot program was limited to the company's twenty-five field sales representatives. After the pilot program proved successful, it was expanded to include the company's more than three hundred independent representatives.

Still another approach is for the consultant to build and operate a prototype and then turn that over to the company. This was the recent experience of a company wanting to expand into Latin America. A prototype center, focused on the Mexican market, was designed, built, and operated by the consultant. After six months of fine-tuning, the center was moved to Mexico City, where it is operated by the company.

Finally, you can have the consultant not only design the center but also operate it. This, of course, requires close cooperation between the consultant and the company. In effect, the consultant becomes an extension of the company's marketing department. This makes the most sense if this type of operation would become political within the company or if it is not supported by core competencies.

Criteria for selecting a consultant. If you decide you need the help of a consultant, you should be selective and look for hard evidence of a good fit with your company. Following are four criteria you should use in selecting a consultant group:

1. *The consultant s culture.* You have to envision the consultant as a seamless extension of your organization. For the off-site telemarketing center, you need to be especially selective because they will be representing you thousands of times each month to your most valuable asset—your customers.

   You need to visit the consultant's organization and see how they treat their clients and their clients' customers. You should sit down with their telemarketing representatives and monitor how they conduct themselves on the phone. You should have access to their quality assurance procedures and measurements.

   The tools and methodologies the consultant uses are going to produce a certain culture and that culture should be compatible with yours.

2. *Replicated culture at client operations.* The consultant must be able to demonstrate they have been able to replicate

their culture for other clients. They should give you evidence they have accomplished this across client bases—whether off-site or on-site.

3. *Documented process.* The consultant group should demonstrate they have a documented process and are not dependent on management or the knowledge base of a few individuals. The documented process should have quality assurance checkpoints and have documented measurements. These help ensure the centers are well-managed and deliver a high level of quality consistently over a long period of time.

4. *Value delivery.* The primary metrics, or standards of measurement, should not be event-based, such as cost per call, calls per hour, etc. In business-to-business marketing, when building a customer community, you are not interested in how many phone calls are made, you are interested in the results. So, you should look for overall performance measurements. Typical criteria includes sales expense-to-revenue (E/R) ratios and quality measurements at the field and customer levels. In other words, you want to see that E/R ratios have declined and that satisfaction levels are high among field salespeople, distributors, dealers, and end users.

Centralized or Decentralized?

Another major decision at the early stages of C^3 planning is whether to centralize or decentralize. The four levels of centralization/decentralization include:

- Centralized with open support—any representative in the center would handle any customer. The representatives do not have assigned customers or other defined areas. Management is at the centralized location. Efficiency is the highest.

- Centralized with dedicated support—representatives have defined areas of involvement. This could be on a regional basis, i.e., one representative is assigned the Southeast region and all inbound calls from that region are routed to that person. Or, this could be on a product basis or some other type of structure. Management is at the centralized location.

- Decentralized with centralized management—representatives are located in the field or regional offices. Their involvement is only with those customers served by their office. Management is from the corporate level. Service hours may include shared customers early or late in the day.

- Decentralized with local management—representatives are located in the field or regional offices with management at the local level.

The basic rule is to centralize all functions to provide greatest productivity unless a compelling reason exists to dedicate resources for higher levels of effectiveness. A scarcity of functional skills necessary to consistently manage and provide leadership in a C^3 may also suggest centralizing.

Organizational Support

The successful C³ needs to be supported by the culture of the organization. A major part of this process is changing the attitudes of people within the organization. A paradigm shift must occur in which the customer's interests are placed first and individual employee satisfaction and productivity are achieved through delivery of value to the customer. Everyone throughout the organization needs to be committed to the vision that it is the customer that drives the business, not internal policies and procedures.

Moving toward a customer service orientation for a business is not an easy process. It requires new ways of thinking about how customer service reps, and other employees who contact customers, use software and networks.[2]

In his article "Customer Service: Lessons from World-Class Companies," Nick McGaughey, managing director of Applied Information, commented, "Implementing a new customer service strategy often involves changing the way employees perform their jobs. Companies soon realize that the organizational complexities of these initiatives far outweigh the technical challenges."

He went on to say, "Unfortunately, at many companies customer service is a fad or slogan and is not viewed as a long-term business priority. At best-of-class companies, however, customer service is not a task assigned solely to the service function; it is the responsibility of all employees."[3]

Customer service is not just a new process, it is a new attitude. An attitude of customer service must permeate the entire organization, from top management to the production line worker. It cannot be supported by lip service or cute slogans. It has to be supported by a management and organizational commitment. For example, one company delivers employee paychecks in envelopes labeled "Brought to You by the Customer."[4]

TELEMARKETING—THE CORE OF THE C³

The telephone plays a major role in the C³. In the planning stages for setting up a center, it is important to understand the impact the phone has on the entire marketing and sales processes. For example, phone contacts supplement and replace the more expensive face-to-face salesperson contact. This is done in a way that does not reduce the effectiveness of the contact. Also, the phone provides the next best means of establishing a dialogue with the customer, which can lead to establishing long-term relationships.

Increased Customer Contact at a Lower Cost

As noted earlier, frequency of contact is a key issue. Studies show the customer does not recall how a contact was made in as short of a time as five days following the contact. But the customer does remember the content.

In the contact area, the C³ is an economic resource. For example, when analyzing direct sales costs, out of 365 days, 200 days may be available for selling. If the average salesperson can make 3.5 sales calls per day, that's 700 face-to-face customer contacts possible during a year.

Now, compare a telemarketing operation, or a C³. A typical telemarketing representative can complete as many as 35 customer contacts per day, (with 27–30 as an acceptable standard), or as much as ten times the number of contacts of a field salesperson. Consider the impact this would have on a company's sales efforts, especially when each contact delivers value-based communication.

The inherent value of telemarketing and the C^3 are they relieve the field sales channel of time-consuming and nonproductive activities. They also provide the customer with a single contact point. For the sales channel, the C^3 can handle such activities as:

- Order entry

- Order status

- Inventory tracking

- Shipping schedules and delivery tracking

- Disseminating information on the company, its products, and its services

- Collecting information about the customer

- Resolving billing and shipping questions

- Providing customer support services

- Setting appointments

- Account management

- Qualifying leads

- Generating leads

This frees salespeople to use their time for more productive activities that advance the sales process and build relationships in a way unique to face-to-face contact. Time spent with the customer becomes more productive as most of the preliminary information has been handled through the C^3. The salesperson can now concentrate on identifying and solving customer business problems or needs.

The Growth of Business-to-Business Telemarketing

The growth in business-to-business telemarketing has been dramatic. Canadian researchers Harrie Vredenburg and Judith Marshall found 73.5 percent of industrial companies using telemarketing use both inbound and outbound telemarketing. However, they commented, "outgoing telemarketing is viewed as offering the largest future growth potential. Outgoing telemarketing offers firms an alternative or complement to the increasingly expensive personal sales visit. . . ."[5]

The role of the telemarketing center has been increasing. Once accorded a low status in a company, customer service has emerged as a key marketing tool. Much of the technology being used today has been available for some time. But, it is only recently that companies have begun to realize the benefits of customer service.

Another aspect of the C^3 is the account management function. As has been stressed before, at every point of contact you should be gathering information/knowledge. Through this you can communicate value and create a bond through that communication.

In one sense, the C^3 is an enabler in the relationship-building process. The ultimate goal should be to empower everyone in the organization to contribute to building relationships and delivering value to the customer.

Constructing the Customer Community Center

The structure of the Customer Community Center can vary depending upon the specific functions you decide to perform in the center. The model shown in Figure 6-3 represents a full-scale C³ that provides account management in addition to managing and coordinating customer inquiries, services, and sales.

The C³ Model

The Customer Community Center provides an organizational structure for implementing the relationship-building process. The C³ model shows the interrelationship of the major functional areas, the database and operations, which are supported by the product or market management group, the printed response group, the technical support group, the field interface group, and the information systems group.

The Database

The purpose of the database, as discussed in Chapter 5, is to deliver greater value to the customer through establishing a central sales- and marketing-oriented information source. The database contains individual customer records of profile information, order history, and customer contact activity. It is the collective memory of the customer relationship and all customer transactions.

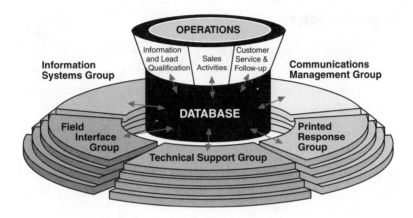

Figure 6-3 Customer Community Center Model

© Hunter Business Direct, Inc.

Operations

The operations portion of the C^3 is shown at the center of the model. This is the core set of functions including information and lead qualification, sales activities, and customer service and follow-up. These are supported by the customer contact database.

This typically is a centralized group of telemarketers who are the primary contact point for customers, resellers, and field sales reps. The C^3 phone reps input and extract data from the marketing database. Using telemarketing offers low-cost, high-frequency, two-way dialogue with customers that continually validates and refreshes the database.

Sizing the Center

Establishing a telemarketing center takes more than just installing phone lines, software, and desks. The first consideration is sizing the operation. This affects equipment issues and people issues.

The primary influence on sizing an operation is the level of phone activity. This includes inbound order taking and inquiry handling, outbound call activity, customer service, and account management. This was discussed earlier in the chapter (see Figure 6-1).

You start with the customer contact plan developed in Chapter 4 and determine the level of value-based communication that the C^3 will be supporting. Then you add the projected number of calls required for sales force support, such as setting up and confirming sales calls. Assuming for budgeting purposes that an outbound telemarketer can complete 25 calls per day, total the number of outbound calls and divide by 6,000, which are the budgeted number of calls per year a telemarketer can make. (Note: Experience shows 27–30 calls can be handled daily. However, it is best to budget on the conservative side to take into account unplanned contingencies.)

This process is repeated for inbound telemarketing. Review the contact log developed in Chapter 4 and then factor in the current number of inquiries you receive and the projected number of inquiries expected from an acquisition program. Then, you can estimate how many inquiries will need to be handled. Continue repeating this process for customer service phone calls, such as billing questions, shipping schedules, and so on.

This process is also extended to other functional areas within the C^3 such as fulfillment, information systems, technical support, etc. Once finished sizing the C^3, and designing an organization structure that supports the functional areas, you can then determine what hardware and software are necessary to support it. This also drives the operating expense and capital expense model.

A sample operating expense and capital expense model is shown in Figure 6-4. This model is for a company selling through a dealer network. All C³ activities focus on dealer contact, both inbound and outbound.

Staffing

Staffing the C³ starts with understanding telemarketer behavior profiles. Three distinct behavioral types are necessary for basic telemarketing functions. Differences exist among outbound telemarketers, inbound telemarketers who handle customer service problems and complaints, and inbound telemarketers who handle order taking, inquiry handling, routine billing and shipping questions, and so on. Since these differences are not just skill sets (which are trainable) but also behaviors (which are not easily changed or trained), it is advisable to hire specialists for each of these areas. The business purpose supported by the phone defines the type of person you need on the phone.

To better understand these difference, in 1995 MPR, Inc. and Hunter Business Direct undertook a study involving in-depth interviews with seventy-two telemarketing employees from four companies. The purpose was to gather data regarding the motivation and behaviors of employees involved in telephone work with the public.

The most important result of the study was salespeople (outbound telemarketers) are more ambitious and competitive

Budget Item	#	Hours	$	Total
Annual Expenses				
1. Staffing				
Operations				
• Phone representatives[1]	35		$27,000	$ 945,000
• Supervisors	4		$37,500	$ 150,000
• Managers	1		$60,000	$ 60,000
• Trainers	1		$37,500	$ 37,500
• Clerical	2		$24,000	$ 48,000
• Database administrator	1		$52,500	$ 52,500
Subtotal Operations	44			$ 1,293,000
Information Systems[2]				
• Analysts	1	1,300	$85/hr	$ 127,500
• Programmers	2	3,000	$55/hr	$ 165,000
• Operator	1	1,500	$40/hr	$ 60,000
Subtotal Information Systems	4	6,000		$ 352,500
Subtotal Staff	48			$ 1,645,500
2. Square footage rental				
• Total number of people	53			53
• Est. space per person (sq. ft.)	48			2,544
• Cost/sq. ft.			$15	
Subtotal				$ 38,160
3. Phone expense				
• Annual inbound volume	400,000		$1.26/each	$ 504,000
• Annual outbound volume	100,000		$1.08/each	$ 108,000
4. Mail expense				
• Postage	300,000		$0.48/each	$ 504,000
• Fulfillment	300,000		$2.00/each	$ 600,000
5. Consulting services		1,000	$100/hr	$ 100,000

6. Other overhead (support services)			$ 708,750
Subtotal Annual Expense			$ 3,848,410

Capital Expense

1. Phone equipment

• Telemarketer phones	35	$250.00	$ 8,750
• Supervisor phones	4	$700.00	$ 2,800
• Regular phones	13	$160.00	$ 2,080
• Leased line			$ 12,000
• Hardware			$ 25,000
• Installation			$ 2,500

2. Computer equipment/software

• CRTs	53	$1,000	$ 53,000
• Hardware			$ 250,000
• Software			$ 435,000
3. Work stations	53	$3,500	$ 185,500
Subtotal Capital Expenses			$ 976,630
Estimated Budget for First Year			$ 4,825,040

[1]Based on call volume requiring 8.0 persons for customer relations, 9.0 for completion status, 8.0 for special programs, and 10.0 for literature requests.

[2]Internal transfer costs

Figure 6-4 C³ Operating and Capital Expense Model

© Hunter Business Direct, Inc.

and service people (inbound telemarketers) are more service-oriented. These are motivational behaviors, which means these are the reasons people come to work and what makes work fulfilling. While other behavioral factors can be learned, motivational factors are so basic to the individual that they are

Inbound

Mission of Service
- Service oriented
- Team player
- Committed to family and community

Responsibility
- Conscientious and dependable
- Good attendance and punctuality
- Committed to delivery of tasks

Empathy
- Sensitive listener
- Recognizes role of human nature in business decisions
- Ready to reach out and comfort

Affiliations
- Enjoys sharing expertise with other professionals
- Contributes to team bonding
- Taps into knowledge in a variety of fields

Achiever
- Confident, self-assured, and very proud of all accomplishments
- Seeks independence and recognition
- Driven to high levels of accomplishment

Intensity
- High stamina and endurance
- Maintains focus during work activities
- Active hobbies

Outbound

Achiever
- Confident, self-assured, and very proud of all accomplishments
- Seeks independence and recognition
- Driven to high levels of performance

Competitor
- Wants to win, hates to lose
- Energized by competition
- Driven to produce

Prospector
- Targets accounts carefully
- Continually probes and penetrates accounts
- Methodically assesses "fit" between prospects and his/her company

Persuader
- Skilled listener who identifies motivations
- Probes and questions others' agendas
- Strives to influence others

Mission of Service
- Service oriented
- Team player
- Committed to family and community

Proactivity
- Looks for solutions
- Initiates change and improvement
- Doesn't blame or shift responsibility

Affiliations
- Enjoys sharing expertise with other professionals
- Contributes to team bonding
- Taps into knowledge in a variety of fields

Figure 6-5 Summary of Traits for Inbound and Outbound Telemarketers

© Hunter Business Direct, Inc.

difficult or impossible to change. So, since behavior cannot be changed, you need to hire individuals based on the function you want them to perform on the phone.

A summary of the study findings[6] are given in Figure 6-5.

This leads to the conclusion that sharing or cross training between these areas is not advisable. People quickly burn out if put into an environment that is not supportive or consistent with their behavior. Primary measurements of performance in each area also prevent crossover between areas. Involuntary telemarketing turnover of 8 percent should be a goal with 12 percent or more considered disastrous. A high correlation exists between employee retention and customer retention.

One issue that arises with staffing is the use of contract or temporary employees. Some people recommend staffing telemarketing centers this way. In business-to-business marketing, this is a prescription for failure. Again, the sales and service community is the heart of the customer community. You cannot expect employees to be loyal to the customer if you are not loyal to them. This is not to say you should not use outside people doing telemarketing. For a telemarketing operation to be successful, you need dedicated people. You can have permanent part-time people, who are trained and regularly included in briefings, but you can't really have a pool of freelance tele-reps on demand and expect to keep the integrity of the relationship.

Diffusing Sales Channel Resistance

Without sales channel support, a telemarketing center is destined for failure. When starting a telemarketing operation, you may encounter resistance or tension between the inside sales/service telemarketers and the field sales channel, whether a salesperson or some other channel member.

Much has been observed and written about the relationship between inside tele-reps and outside sales representatives. In some organizations, the rivalry and tension lead to underutilization of the telemarketing operation and the company sees little improvement in sales productivity. Some of the more common reasons for the reluctance of field sales to embrace a telemarketing operation include:

- *Inherent fear of telemarketing*—Many salespeople have the inherent fear telemarketing will replace them.

- *Fear of increased measurement or conflicting/competitive measures*—Salespeople are unaccustomed to having their performance analyzed, outside of gross sales figures, and so on. Now salespeople and sales channels are more accountable for their activities.

- *Fear of encroachment on MY territory*—Salespeople tend to be independent and possessive, they do not want anyone "interfering" in their "space," or territory. This attitude of protectionism can seriously affect the success of telemarketing.

- *Losing control of the customer*—Most salespeople believe they are the primary reason the customer buys from the company and don't want anyone else contacting their customer and jeopardizing that relationship. This can especially be true of channel partners, such as distributors or rep organizations, who are independent sales operations and may be reluctant to reveal who their customers and prospects are.

- *Someone else defining success or failure*—In conventional operations, sales success is typically measured using some type of gross sales quota system. Now, success is measured along other dimensions, such as customer retention, increasing lifetime value, building loyalty, obtaining referrals, account penetration, product penetration, lead closures, and so on.

This initial reluctance can be replaced with enthusiasm provided you involve field sales representatives in the planning and design process. Once a field salesperson sees how much more efficient they can become and how the telemarketer provides the salesperson with support, extending his or her ability to service customers, these attitudes change. Also, and probably of greater importance, salespeople quickly see this increases their ability to make money. In the community centers built and operated for Hewlett-Packard, Toshiba, Shell, and Lexmark, field sales representatives and inside telemarketers have developed effective relationships that lead to stronger customer ties.

Sales Force Automation

Field salespeople must have access to the customer database in order to take advantage of the relationship-building tools available through the C^3. When a salesperson has timely and complete contact information, she or he can deliver additional leveraged value when having a face-to-face contact with the customer.

Consider the following scenario:

Jack sells electrical test equipment used by manufacturers of equipment that use electric motors. A variety of industries are involved. Jack's territory includes three Midwestern states and a portion of a fourth state. Within his territory are twelve major population centers with a high density of manufacturing. Jack has more than 200 active customers. Forty of these companies are a source of continuing business for Jack and an additional sixty companies appear to be growing. The remainder are occasional purchasers of equipment.

Jack's company just introduced a new product and he is scheduling visits to the twelve cities in his territory over the next six weeks. He plans to spend four days each week in the field and expects to make three sales calls per day. Each morning, he drags out his customer files and pulls the files for the appointments he has scheduled for the day. He reviews his notes on each account and proceeds to his first meeting.

Jack begins his first meeting with Doug, who is responsible for test and quality operations at a fast-growing conveyor manufacturing company. Jack reacquaints himself with Doug and then begins reviewing the new product. Doug does not recall receiving a product announcement so Jack digs out the sales brochure and begins to cover the particulars of the product. As Jack describes the pertinent features, Doug has some questions, which quickly leads to the conclusion the new test product does not meet his needs. However, he tells Jack the company recently changed motor suppliers and has some new test functions.

After some additional time spent probing Doug for more particulars, Jack believes an existing product would meet Doug's new needs. Doug is interested and wants a quote. Jack says he will get that to Doug but has to first verify prices with the home office. At this point, Doug is pressed for time and asks Jack to send him some information and a quote. Jack doesn't get the opportunity to completely review how the test product would solve Doug's specific requirements.

Contrast this with Sally's experience. Sally is with Jack's competitor and has the same territory as Doug. She is scheduled to meet with Doug because two weeks ago the telemarketing representative spoke with Doug and learned about the new motors. At that point Bill, the telemarketing rep, probed Doug for particulars and determined Doug's new criteria for test equipment. Bill then faxed product information to Doug on one of the company's products that might meet Doug's needs and discussed this with Sally in their daily phone conversation. Sally then requested a meeting be set up with Doug.

Now, Sally is in her hotel room and uses her laptop connected to a modem to call the company's marketing database. It automatically updates her computer files. Next, Sally checks Doug's file and finds Bill reconfirmed her meeting and learned Doug had invited Charley, his boss, to also meet with Sally.

When Sally meets with Doug and Charley, they are able to immediately begin discussing the specific issues related to the new motors. Doug has had an opportunity to review the product literature and now Sally can highlight those features that best solve Doug's problem. Doug asks for a quote and Sally accesses her laptop and gives Doug the latest pricing information along with product availability and projected delivery dates.

When Sally leaves Doug's office, she uses her cellular phone and calls a voice mailbox to report the outcome of her call and any other pertinent information that should be added to Doug's database. She also wants Charley added to the

database. She then asks for a quote to be prepared and provides the details. Later that morning, Doug receives a faxed
formal quote along with a personal note expressing Sally and
Bill's interest in working with Doug.

Sally's approach to selling is how business-to-business
salespeople are increasing their productivity and building
relationships with customers by delivering greater value. In
Jack's case, he wasted Doug's time by reviewing information
that had no value to Doug. Then, when Jack finally uncovered Doug's real needs, he ran out of time.

The time spent by Jack getting to the point of understanding the problem was handled by Sally's telemarketing rep in a
single phone call. This was a preplanned phone call and Doug
was expecting it since the telemarketing rep had established
when Doug preferred to be called. When Doug knew Sally was
coming to see him, he knew she would be prepared to discuss
specific issues of concern to him so was willing to invite others
into the meeting. Again, this becomes the case of establishing a
reputation for value-based contacts with the customer.

While the costs associated with supplying a sales force with
laptop computers, the necessary software, and training can
seem high, the payoff is usually worth the investment. According to the Conference Board, initial costs can be recovered
within the first two years.[7]

However, just giving salespeople laptops does not give
you an automatic boost in sales productivity. You need to
have sales force input into the basic decisions related to
automation. You need to provide adequate training to ensure
salespeople realize the potential benefits of automation.

Allen Levin, managing principal with Decision Support Technology, told the story of a large, multi-line insurance company that bought 1,000 laptops for its sales force several years ago. He related, "They got all these laptops, they dumped about 10 software packages into each one—the word processor, the spreadsheet and everything else—and they shipped out the boxes to the offices. Then they all went back to work. Salespeople who tried to figure out what was going on actually reduced their productivity. They just dumped a bunch of hardware and software. It had nothing to do with helping the salespeople. Nobody even talked to the salespeople."[8]

Laptop or portable computers open entire new vistas for salespeople. With the addition of CD-ROM devices to some laptops, salespeople can now have multimedia product presentations at their fingertips. But, keep in mind, technology is not the issue. It is the functional use of the technology that contributes to sales productivity and enhanced customer relationships.

Compensation

Rewards and recognition are a key factor in the success of a C^3. Inside salespeople need to believe they are valued and are contributing as much as the outside salesperson. This means compensation programs must similarly reward both inside and outside salespeople. They should be based on results that allow telesales to complement field sales goals.

One group of researchers, writing in the *Journal of Business & Industrial Marketing*, saw the structure of sales force compensation systems as contributing to difficulties when implementing relationship marketing. They noted compensation has been one of the more important issues in sales force management. Incentive plans for field salespeople typically stress improving motivation of the individual sales person. Since the salesperson is rewarded for individual performance, this conflicts with relationship building, which involves support from within the company to service customers.

Their study found that the people upon whom the salesperson relies for customer support may be less committed to customer service when the reward and compensation systems do not take into account their contribution to the sales process. The study also found a group compensation system has problems as its reward structure does not recognize individual effort.[9]

One troubling aspect of field sales compensation is many companies rely solely on commission-based compensation. This does not encourage relationship building, but encourages transaction-based selling.

It is important that telemarketing sales representatives and field sales representatives have compensation systems that reward them for the same results. This is not to say each should be rewarded equally. Rather, each should participate in the compensation for sales and increased customer satisfaction and retention. A number of different formulas have proven successful, but one of the more imaginative, and effective, is one developed by a company that manufactures wooden dowel rods and sells to home service companies.

Their compensation program rewards both the field salesperson and the telemarketing representative using an interesting formula. In their system, at the beginning of each year the field salesperson selects the top 100 accounts in their territory. On those accounts, the salesperson earns 7 percent commission on all revenues. On any other account, the salesperson earns 3 percent. The telemarketing representative then earns 5 percent commission on all the accounts not selected by the salesperson, and 2 percent on revenues from the accounts the salesperson picked. Each has a stake in seeing that the other does well.

With this system, the telemarketing rep knows that supporting the salesperson translates into dollars and that any other business he or she generates earns money. The salesperson is recognized for his or her ability and would not be averse to contacting an account not in their selected 100 since a commission is still earned on the sale the telemarketing representative may get.

Physical Design

Design the workplace to deliver high employee productivity and satisfaction. The job design should be developed to support the workplace environment, which supports internal service values. Internal service values are those that contribute to employee satisfaction, retention, and productivity. Above all else, the physical design should enable the people to deliver value to the customer.

Marketing consultants Rapp and Collins described their visit to Fidelity Investments' telemarketing as a major revelation. They were anticipating phone reps to be jammed into tiny cubicles. Instead, at the company's Boston headquarters,

"The reps were in a bright, cheery area, two stories high, with a 100-foot window wall revealing a panoramic view of Boston Harbor. It is the managers who are occupying interior offices without a window."[10]

Measurement

Measurement is an integral part of the C^3. For the numbers to make sense, you need to know *what* to measure. Measurement has to be based on effectiveness; i.e., how many calls does the telemarketing representative save the field salesperson from making on each active account.

Measurement systems for business-to-business telemarketing do not look like they do in the consumer environment. Consumer measurements are interested in transactions, i.e., number of calls, number of mail pieces, etc. The focus is on cost per transaction such as response rates, cost per call, calls per telemarketer, cost per thousand names, etc.

This does not work in business-to-business marketing. Rather, loyalty and quality are the key measurements. The results that are meaningful are defection and retention rates, target market share, and sales increases from product penetration and account penetration.

Measuring telemarketers' performance cannot be based on the number of phone calls a representative makes, except as a part of a process. The key is leveraging the higher cost of field sales. One way to measure performance is through sales expense-to-revenue ratios for the entire sales operation.

Effectiveness Research Results

Canadian educators Judith Marshall and Harrie Vredenburg conducted a study of 385 sales and marketing managers in industrial companies that had outbound telemarketing programs for sales support or as a sales channel. The study looked at the effectiveness of the telemarketing operations.

The study found most companies considered telemarketing to be supplemental to field sales and not a replacement for field sales. Nearly all the companies surveyed (94.4 percent) had their own sales force. Only two companies used telemarketing as their only sales channel.

The study found those firms that had increased their use of telemarketing and had increased the number of telemarketing representatives reported the greatest success. Similarly, the same pattern emerged for those reporting moderate success or not very successful operations. For example, those reporting not very successful telemarketing results also reported a decreasing use of telemarketing and a decrease in the number of telemarketing reps.

Another significant difference emerged between companies employing full-time telemarketing representatives and those where telemarketing reps spend only part of their time on telemarketing. Of the very successful companies, 80 percent made telemarketing a major part of the representative's job. In the not very successful group of companies, 57.7 percent included telemarketing as one task among many an employee performed.

According to the study's authors, "This finding suggests that even if a company is implementing a small telemarketing operation, it is probably a better strategy not to spread tele-marketing responsibilities too thinly, but to make telemarket-ing tasks a major part of the job for one or two people who can then become telemarketing specialists."[11]

In the compensation area, the study reported 53.8 per-cent paid salary only to telemarketing representatives while the rest paid a bonus or commission in addition to a base salary. A higher percentage reporting very successful telemar-keting paid some salary/bonus combination—54.8 percent compared to 45.2 percent who paid salary only. A very high proportion of not very successful companies paid salary only (75.9 percent).[12]

As one can see, the operations portion of the C^3 (Figure 6-3) requires careful planning. In addition, five other functions or organizational interfaces within the database naturally develop in a community center.

COMMUNICATIONS MANAGEMENT GROUP

In the C^3, the Communications Management Group develops integrated marketing campaigns for the company. This group does not have to be centrally located, but it does help. The group takes input from business units or product/brand man-agers on types of marketing programs they need. The group coordinates the implementation of programs with all other groups (where necessary). This is a key group as it controls the message being delivered, and designs campaigns and con-tact plans. Specific tasks of this group include the following.

Design and Develop Literature

A primary responsibility is to put together the value-based communication materials that will be sent to the customer. They work closely with the customer contact plan and determine which literature will be sent with what mailing.

Define Telemarketing Guide Objectives

Scripts are common in consumer telemarketing. These are carefully crafted and the telemarketer is expected to follow them to the letter. However, this is not the case in business-to-business marketing. Here, the telemarketer is provided with objectives to be accomplished during a call in the form of a guide for topics/subjects to cover. This results in a more interactive, responsive, and free-flowing business type communication—not a scripted communication.

Determine Measures

The most powerful selects used in business-to-business marketing to drive customer loyalty and retention of customers are what's now being determined by the Harvard Business School and the cutting-edge people in the service industry—recency, frequency, amount, and referrals. These are the business drivers. These are the quantifiable measurements most highly correlated to retention of customers.

Develop Lead Generation Programs

Lead generation programs are implemented by the Communications Management Group. You need to understand who your customers are and who your prospects are with selectable attributes. The strategic plan defines the target market and the selects within that target market that you are going to go after.

Design Standard Personalized Letters

Working with operations, this group helps prepare personalized letter messages and formats. The power of working with a database is you can target segments to receive marketing letters personalized to the interest level of the segment.

For example, the ideal approach would be to develop printed materials, such as brochures, for each market segment. In that way, you could tailor the message of the brochure to meet the unfulfilled needs of that particular segment. However, the cost for this would not be justified in business-to-business marketing. Rather, you create a feature-rich, benefit-oriented marketing brochure and then individualize the cover letter to address specific needs of each market segment. In that way you are, in effect, tailoring the brochure to the needs of the segment.

Design and Analyze Measurement Reports

This group is also responsible for developing and analyzing measurement reports.

Program Training and Instruction

Another role this group has is to keep the representatives on the phone current on product or service features and applications.

This can include new product training, case history reviews, and sharing information gained through customer contacts.

To show how this group operates, consider the communications involved with a trade show. Building traffic flow at exhibits, trade shows, seminars, and similar events leverages the presence of field salespeople. It is a natural use of integrated mail and phone to find prospects most likely to be interested in the event message and then to document a clearer understanding of the attendee's needs and perception of the products and services. This information is also often valuable in market research. Ideally, you want the "right" people to come to a specific event. Once you identify who will be attending, you can focus on pinpointing their needs and aligning the event and messages to meet those needs.

You should understand an attendee's needs with enough clarity that you can collect background material and plan face-to-face meetings with individuals at the event. This type of pre-event contact often leads to increased efficiency and effectiveness of the event, as well as increased foot traffic.

Event follow-up is also important. A limited number of new prospect contacts will be prequalified that justify immediate field sales follow-up. Typically, most companies let the remaining contacts drop through the cracks. With a database system, a majority of these attendees can be sorted into active and inactive status. Those active ones are qualified over a period of time to determine whether they are, in fact, appropriate for future field follow-up. It is economically appropriate that specific communications, including literature and samples, be managed through an integrated mail and phone follow-up system as additional qualification steps.

Printed Response Group

Within the C³, this group performs all mail room functions for printed material or personalized letters and response material. The group will stock, mail, and reorder literature supplies and other support materials, such as videotapes, audio tapes, premiums, diskettes, CDs, and so on. Printed material will be created by the Communications Management Group. Personalized letters will be generated from Operations.

Technical Support Group

This group will answer technically specific questions from customers, end users, or channel distributors that are beyond the experience of "frontline" communicators. Customers known to have special technical needs can be given a special (back door) phone number for direct access to this group. Other customers calling the central information phone number would be transferred to this group only if the answer to their question has not been previously documented.

The answers to all questions taken by this group will be entered into the Central Marketing Database for general access by all groups. This type of information can also be a source of information for newsletters and other mailings of value-based communication. The Technical Support Group can also direct the Printed Response Group in fulfillment of technical literature.

Field Interface Group

This group provides a central, personal contact for dealers, jobbers, franchises, national accounts, sales reps, wholesalers, and retailers to interface with the C³. It supports sales management functions to coordinate account planning activities between the customer, field sales reps, and telephone contact. It distributes and manages qualified leads and reports, account management information, and other sales interfaces.

INFORMATION SYSTEMS GROUP

This group supports and has responsibility for the functionality of the electronic communication networks and the centralized database. The group will maintain the internal network linking together all functional groups with the database, i.e., inventory, order processing status, accounting, etc.

This group is also responsible for selecting and supporting the software used for the C³. At a minimum, the software should support these specific functions:

- Compile a combined marketing contact database from all business units
- Related accounting functions
- Track products and programs
- Report results
- Gather sales and customer data from all functional groups
- Provide multiple selects of stored data
- Generate personalized letters

It is through the C³ that you will be able to build sustainable relationships with the customer. These relationships lead to building a customer community, which is based on economic advantages for you and your customers. When you use this approach to business-to-business marketing, you reduce the cost of sales, make your field sales force more effective and productive, build lasting customer relationships, and increase revenues and profitability.

COMMUNITY BUILDING IN ACTION: BUSINESSFORMS

BusinessForms is now ready to build their Customer Community Center. Step one is to identify the contact points they have with their customers. This includes all sales channels. Contact log sheets have been recorded at all sites in the customer service areas of the company, the accounting/collection area, the order center, the inquiry center, etc. The account management Customer Contact Matrix in manufacturing, government, and health care adds additional capacity and competency requirements. Total volumes and contact types are logged in a matrix by contact point. Careful analysis now marks those functions and communications for inclusion in the C^3.

The C^3 development team begins to see the magnitude of the project and also sees many of the pieces are already in place. Their job now is to bring together what they already have running into a new, coordinated center, focusing on the needs of the customer to drive communications. Account management is new, as is lead management, so these are woven into the new center.

The center is sized around volumes, functions, and competencies defined in the project workpapers. With careful consideration, the development team defines the roles, specifies the positions, determines performance requirements, and documents measurements. Employees are screened and selected based on behavior as well as experience and personal chemistry.

This process must involve key field sales representatives who have demonstrated leadership and influence in the field. Their enthusiastic support is captured in weekly sales conference calls and the newsletter. They must feel ownership of this program. Only then can they clearly communicate its value to other field sales representatives and to their customers. They realize this is a new way of doing business that is required to remain competitive. And, they are convinced it helps increase their value to the customer.

The C^3 is now ready for a six-month pilot program. The product managers begin to coordinate their messages and focus on what the customers are saying they value. During the first three months of the pilot program, literature volume drops 35 percent. Second and third callbacks drop dramatically so that overall volume per order shipped drops 8 percent. Customer surveys show service levels are up and overall sales expense-to-revenue goes down 7 percent.

At the end of the pilot program, BusinessForms is convinced the design of the C^3 will work and they move it from a pilot program to a full-scale community center.

Notes

1. Joseph Cosco, "The Razor's Edge," *The Journal of Business Strategy*, November/December 1993, 60.

2. Ibid.

3. Nick McGaughey, "Customer Service: Lessons from World-

Class Companies," *Industrial Engineering,* March 1993, 20.

4. Frederick F. Reichheld, "Loyalty-Based Management," *Harvard Business Review,* March–April 1993, 64.

5. Harrie Vredenburg, and Judith J. Marshall, "A Field Experimental Investigation of a Social Influence Application in Industrial Marketing Communication Strategy," *Journal of Direct Marketing* 5:3, Summer 1991, 8.

6. MPR, Inc.

7. William C. Moncrief III, Charles W. Lamb, Jr., and Jane M. Mackay, "Laptop Computers in Industrial Sales," *Industrial Marketing Management* 20, 1991, 280.

8. Priscilla C. Brown, "No Quick Fix," *Business Marketing,* September 1992, 91.

9. Dean Tjosvold, Lindsay Meredith, and R. Michael Wellwood, "Implementing Relationship Marketing: A Goal Interdependence Approach," *Journal of Business & Industrial Marketing,* 1993, 13.

10. Stan Rapp and Thomas L. Collins, *Beyond MaxiMarketing: The New Power of Caring and Daring* (New York: McGraw-Hill, 1994), 167–169.

11. Judith J. Marshall and Harrie Vredenburg. "Successfully Using Telemarketing in Industrial Sales," *Industrial Marketing Management* 17, 1988, 20.

12. Ibid.

7

RETAINING AND CULTIVATING EXISTING CUSTOMERS

A well-known principle of marketing is that the best sources for new business are your current customers. To this end, you *cultivate* your existing customers for additional business. Cultivation is a powerful tool for customer retention and profitable growth.

The strategies used in cultivation have similarities with the strategies used for new customer acquisition, which are covered in Chapter 8. At times, the line between cultivation and acquisition blurs. Keep in mind, this is part of an integrated process and separating the two is, at best, an artificial label on a continuum of cultivation activities on prospects that look like your best customers. For planning and economic modeling, customer acquisition begins with that point on the continuum where the cost of revenue generation makes its most dramatic increase.

To illustrate the importance of cultivation and retention, consider the results of a recent survey of two hundred companies, which found:[1]

- 80 percent reported having a formal system to contact customers on a regular basis.

- Only 11 percent knew the lifetime value of their customers.

- Only 10 percent had a system to alert them when a customer is about to stop doing business with them.

Regarding frequency of customer contact, the study reported:

- 10 percent never.

- 20 percent 3+ times.

- 40 percent 1 or 2 times.

- 30 percent didn't know.

- 40 percent knew how many customers they lose per year.

- 90 percent had a system to find out why a customer left.

An interesting aspect of this study is 90 percent of the executives surveyed had no means of determining when a customer was about to defect. Yet, 90 percent claimed they had a system in place to determine why the customer left.

Cultivation, then, encompasses a number of activities directly related to customer retention and loyalty. It includes:

- synchronized, value-based customer contact focusing on building the relationship;

- increasing the frequency, recency, and dollar amount of orders from existing individual customers, buyer groups, locations, and accounts;

- using customer referrals to embrace apostles and build new relationships at various levels of the customer organization;

- listening and responding to customer complaints and using that information to reduce your customers at risk;

- reactivating dormant customers by resolving the reasons they defected or became dormant;

- continuously monitoring and measuring customer attitudes through customer behavior and surveys.

In the Integrated Marketing Model, shown in Figure 7-1, the lower portion shows the conceptual framework for retaining and cultivating existing customers. The upper portion covers acquisition, discussed in Chapter 8.

In the lower path (Customer Retention), with the exception of the last two items—strengthening the relationship and measurement—the other activities have been discussed in previous chapters. The cultivation process supports customer retention and enables you to build on and expand your relationship with the customer to increase revenues and profits.

LOYAL CUSTOMERS LEAD TO NEW BUSINESS

Customer cultivation centers around the simple economics that an existing, loyal customer provides a steady stream of revenue and represents a lower-cost opportunity for additional business. The better customers know you, and you

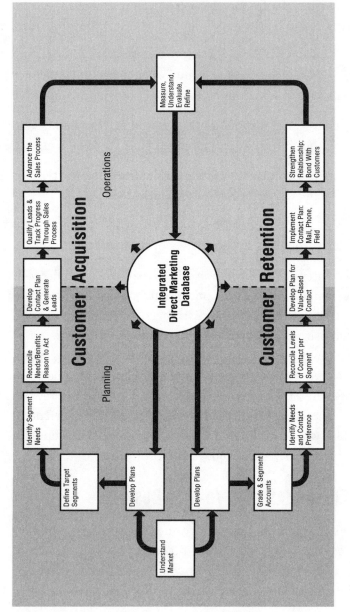

Figure 7-1 Integrated Marketing Model

know them, the more likely they will continue to buy from you. That is one reason the contact plan, developed in Chapter 4, emphasizes increasing account contact frequency. The more frequent you are in value-based contact with the customer, the better you get to know them and the better they get to know you. It's the frequency of value-based contacts, not the contact medium, that has the greatest impact on improving perceived service levels.

THE CULTIVATION PROCESS

Cultivation encompasses all the activities in the retention model shown in Figure 7-1. It involves the initial actions of defining what the customer values in the relationship, understanding customer preferences for information and contact media, delivering value with each contact with the customer, and listening and responding to customer complaints. In practice, this implements the Contact Matrix developed in Chapter 4 (Figure 4-7), which is a synchronized and planned communication program delivering value to the customer at every point of contact.

The fundamental objectives in cultivation are to increase product line penetration and the number of buyers within the customer's organization. You, in effect, want to *penetrate* all levels of the customer's organization.

The starting point is the database, which, as discussed in Chapter 5, is structured around the individual. The construction of the database starts with the individual customer's name, their functional or application area, i.e., buying group, location, and corporate organization. Each one of these categories represents an opportunity for additional business. This penetration process, or *harvesting* the relationship, can be visualized using the Account Cube Model (Figure 7-2).

The Account Cube Model covers the strategies of product penetration, buyer group penetration, and location penetration. In the model (1) represents product penetration at the individual buyer level, (2) is buyer penetration within the buyer's functional group, (3) is location penetration with other functional groups at the buyer's location, and (4) is penetrating other locations within the buyer's organization.

(1) Product Penetration

The first step in this penetration strategy is to increase product line penetration at the individual buyer level (1). If you have listened to the customer, you will have discovered unmet or unfulfilled needs that can lead to additional product or service sales the customer may already buy from someone else or will accept as a related or new product or service.

A good example of this, which ties together many of the attributes of the database, involves Amoco's marketing of Atlas-branded products. The Amoco database had detailed product information, not just product category information. It also had each service station segmented by individual mechanics and service bays.

One way Amoco used the database was to periodically review product sales. In one instance they noted shock absorber sales were relatively flat. They then extracted the buying history of those mechanics who installed the most shock absorbers and found a correlation between tires and

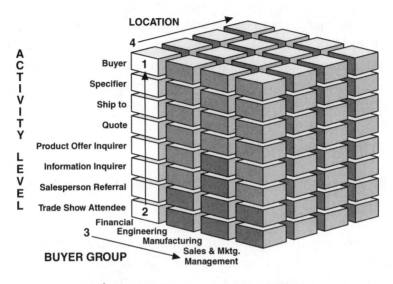

Figure 7-2 The Account Cube Model

© Hunter Business Direct, Inc.

shock absorbers. They found, on an average, one shock absorber was installed for every twelve tires, yet, given industry ratios, they expected one shock absorber for every four tires.

With this information, Amoco developed a product penetration program that involved educating mechanics on how to quickly check for shock absorber wear. This included covering shock absorbers as part of the scheduled phone contact with the service station and having field sales representatives conduct brief training sessions during their scheduled field sales contacts. The result was a steady increase in shock absorber installations.

It is important to note that needs must be attached to a business problem. Sometimes a customer will express a desire for a product feature or service, but if that feature or service does not contribute to the solution of a business problem, you run the risk of mistaking a "wish" for a need. Satisfying a business need adds value to the customer's operation. Satisfying a wish simply gratifies the customer's ego. You need to focus on customer needs for economic survival.

(2) Buyer Group Penetration

Increased individual buyer loyalty leads to the next step, expanding your customer community to include other customers within the individual's organization. A loyal customer will refer you to others within their organization. As has been noted time and time again, the best source for new business is your current customer. This is the payoff of the cultivation strategy.

First, you ask the customer about other individuals within the buyer group who may have the same application for your products or services, represented by (2) in the model. This presumes the customer is knowledgeable about your products or services and their potential applications. If you have been diligent and effective in your value-based communications, the customer will have this knowledge.

For example, consider the case of a laptop computer manufacturer who sells a laptop computer to a partner with a national accounting firm in their tax practice. The company would have already contacted the customer to determine what other products or services fit his or her business application. This might include accessories such as battery recharger, carrying case, additional disk storage, etc.

Now, buyer group penetration involves asking the customer to refer you to other people within the tax practice. In other words, the satisfied customer is providing qualified new business leads.

(3) Location Penetration

Location penetration, represented by (3), involves going beyond the buyer's functional group and penetrating other functions at the buyer's location. In this instance, you have your customer give you referrals to other functional areas at his or her location.

Returning to the laptop computer example, after the company has contacted those potential buyers with the accounting firm's tax practice, now they ask the customer to refer them to other practices within the firm, at the customer's location. This would then involve contacting partners in other areas such as contracts, intellectual property, corporate securities, litigation, and so on.

(4) Other Location Penetration

The next logical step is to look beyond the buyer's location to other plants, offices, or sites the buyer's organization may have, represented by (4). Using the laptop computer example, this means gaining referrals to the accounting firm's other offices. The objective is to find new buyers with the same business applications as the current buyers. In this case, the most logical place to start would be the tax practice departments in other locations.

By penetrating the account cube, you broaden product line sales and find new customers at a lower cost than growing business outside your customer base. Using a penetration strategy refocuses you on the needs of existing customers.

This increases customer loyalty. Therefore, this penetration strategy delivers a double benefit—it's a low cost way of growing the business and it creates more loyalty with existing customers.

PRODUCT LIFE CYCLE ACCELERATION

Another facet of cultivation is it contributes to increased revenue on the standard product life cycle. In today's highly competitive business environment, abbreviated product life cycles are becoming the norm. For example, some personal computer manufacturers measure their product life cycles in months, not years. With market segments shrinking and product life cycles getting shorter, getting product into sales channels quicker has significant competitive advantage. The impact of accelerating product introductions with a well-developed cultivation program can be seen in Figure 7-3.

Three aspects of this need discussion. First is faster product introduction. P_1 is the traditional product life cycle and P_2 is the accelerated product life cycle. By shortening the product introduction time, you achieve incremental sales revenues, represented by R_1.

For example, Toshiba cut their new product introduction time from more than eight weeks to about five days through an integrated communication plan. Using their database, Toshiba can contact every key decision maker, by fax or the telephone, in every location inside every key account within a week. The result is the early stages of the product life cycle have a faster growth path.

The second aspect is the accelerated product life cycle has a higher amplitude than the traditional one. Thus, R_2 shows the incremental revenues resulting from this higher

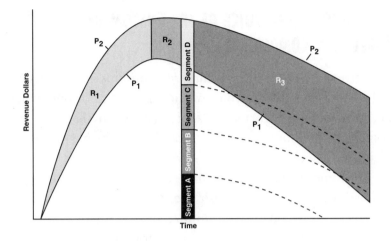

Figure 7-3 Product Life Cycle Acceleration

© Hunter Business Direct, Inc.

amplitude, which can be extended throughout the rest of the product life cycle.

The final aspect comes from the effects of a targeted mature product strategy. When the product life cycle (P_2) reaches the end of R_2, you stop and analyze the market segments and develop strategies to extend the life cycle within all segments. These strategies include account and product penetration at each location and new customer acquisition. For example, if Segment A represented accountants at independent accounting firms who wanted low-cost, number-crunching laptops, then Toshiba would target that segment and cultivate it with powerful black-and-white monitors.

The net result of focusing on the individual segments within the product life cycle is a slower rate of decay. The sum of each of these new, more encouraging, revenue curves is a significant increase in revenue during the later stages of the product life cycle (R_3).

LISTENING TO THE VOICE OF THE CUSTOMER– ESPECIALLY COMPLAINTS

Effective cultivation and building relationships is not possible unless you listen to the voice of the customer, not only when actively seeking information, but also when the customer complains. Without complaints, you lose a valuable means for identifying potentially business-threatening problems.

Customer defections are anathema to business. While it is impossible, and not even desirable, to prevent all defections, steps should be taken to minimize defections of good customers. One step is to establish a program to record, handle, and resolve customer complaints, and feed back information for improvement.

Remember, not all defections are bad. For example, it is better to lose a bad customer, or one that does not fit into your customer community, than to expend resources to salvage the customer and put good customers at risk.

The Value of Complaints

A study, by Claes Fornell of the University of Michigan and Birger Wernerfelt of Northwestern University, showed maximizing the number of complaints from dissatisfied customers (subject to cost constraints) is in the best interest of the firm. This finding appears to be contrary to common business practice. Yet, it has proven to be the best means of identifying customers-at-risk.

The study further showed the firm often is well advised to compensate dissatisfied buyers with amounts exceeding the product's contribution to overhead. Finally, it showed, by attracting and resolving complaints, the firm can defend against competitive advertising and lower the cost of offensive marketing without losing market share.[2]

In a situation where the customer has a problem, four possible actions can occur:

- The customer complains and is satisfied with the response.

- The customer complains and is mollified, but not completely satisfied, with the response.

- The customer complains and is not satisfied with the response.

- The customer does not complain and remains dissatisfied.

A number of studies show the impact of these actions. For example, John Goodman of TARP, who studied the complaint process at over three hundred companies and government agencies, concluded customers who complain to headquarters about routine problems represent a tiny fraction of all dissatisfied customers, somewhere between 2 and 4 percent. The majority of the dissatisfied keep quiet because they don't think complaining will be worthwhile; while others tell their problems in passing to friends or to sales and service people, but not to the customer service department, the only place that keeps track of complaints.[3]

Another TARP study shows the reasons people do not complain include:

- It is not worth the hassle.

- They do not know where or how to complain.

- They do not believe the company will do anything.

This study shows how serious the management of the complaint process can be:

- 80 percent complain to a sales representative or phone representative (frontline employee) and, of those complaints, 75 percent are satisfied and 25 percent are not satisfied.

- Of those dissatisfied, one in five complain to middle management and 80 percent are satisfied.

- Half of those still dissatisfied complain to top management.

- Top management gets three complaints.

When you extrapolate these figures, you find the three complaints to top management have the following implications:

- Six complaints to middle management not satisfactorily resolved

- 30 complaints to middle management due to the failure of frontline employees to satisfactorily resolve them

- 150 complaints to frontline employees not satisfactorily resolved

- 600 total complaints

- 750 total customer problems

The type of product involved also plays a role in the complaint process. Some recent TARP data shows a difference between complaints received for small-ticket items and large-ticket items. It shows 96 percent of customers who experience a problem with a small-ticket item don't complain and 63 percent don't buy again (with small-ticket service, it's 45 percent and 45 percent respectively). With large-ticket items, 27 percent don't complain and 41 percent won't buy again (for large-ticket service items, it's 37 percent and 50 percent respectively).

The TARP data also shows a customer whose small-ticket complaint is dealt with satisfactorily will tell five other people. The figure moves to eight for large-ticket items. When customers' complaints are dealt with to their satisfaction, they resolve to buy again—92 percent in the case of small-ticket items and up to 70 percent for large-ticket items.

Effectively Resolving Complaints

As the studies and data show, complaints adversely affect any type of retention strategy a company may have. In order to retain customers, one needs to stem the flow of defectors through a strategic complaint management. Not just good listening but also appropriate and responsible action.

An obvious step is a toll-free number to make it easy for the customer to contact you. Yet, it is amazing the number of industrial companies that resist using toll-free numbers because they look at them strictly as an expense. The investment in an 800 or 888 number has proven to deliver significant payoffs in identifying problems and saving customers.

The next factor to consider is the timeliness of a response rather than the content of the response. For example, if you respond quickly, the customer has more confidence in you than if you put them off and come back with a better solution. A timely response, even if it does not completely resolve the complaint, shows the customer you are interested in remedying the situation and you value the relationship.

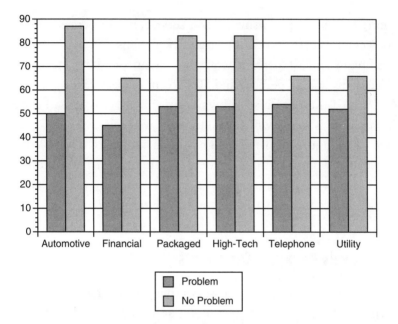

Figure 7-4 Impact of Problem Experience on Loyalty

Source: John Goodman, Scott M. Broetzmann, and Dianne S. Ward, "Preventing TQM Problems: Measured Steps Toward Customer-Driven Quality Improvement," *National Productivity Review*, Autumn 1993, 558. Used with permission of TARP.

Another consideration is: Who answers the phone when a customer complains? You want people who are enthusiastic about hearing complaints on the phone, who understand and have a behavior that lets them listen to customers and solve customer problems. As was mentioned before, one of Stephen Covey's seven habits is "seek first to understand." This is critical in dealing with dissatisfied customers.

Getting customers to complain, and then solving those complaints, actually produces a significant lift in retention and an economic return far greater than problem handling costs.

In an article authored by John Goodman, Scott M. Broetz-

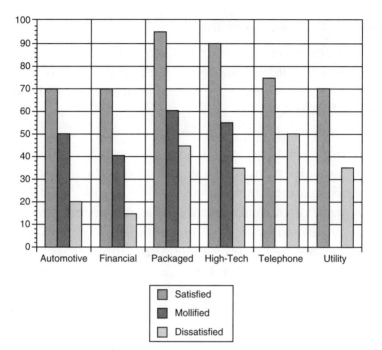

Figure 7-5 Impact of Complaint Experience on Loyalty

Source: John Goodman, Scott M. Broetzmann, and Dianne S. Ward, "Preventing TQM Problems: Measured Steps Toward Customer-Driven Quality Improvement," *National Productivity Review,* Autumn 1993, 559. Used with permission of TARP.

mann, and Dianne S. Ward, all with TARP, they noted, "The payback from problem prevention can be quantified by examining the impact of problems on customer loyalty. Across most industries, problem experience reduces customer loyalty by 10 to 20 percent. Expressed another way, for every six customers who perceive they have had an unpleasant surprise, you risk losing some, if not all, of the future revenue from at least one of those six customers."[4] Figures 7-4 and 7-5 show the potential impact of problem prevention and complaint handling on customer loyalty in several industries.

Complaints Enhance Retention

Listening to customer problems and resolving them has additional benefits. It leads to developing new products or offering new services that enhance customer retention and loyalty because a complaint can also be indicative of new unfulfilled customer needs.

Many companies are recognizing the complaining customer provides them with valuable information. One company that takes this information seriously is Hewlett-Packard. Every piece of customer feedback is assigned to an "owner" at HP, who must act on the information and respond to the person who called. For example, if a customer has a complaint about an HP printer, the person assigned to the call will first check the company's database to see how widespread the particular complaint is. The database also contains information on what action is being taken to resolve the problem. This gives the "owner" valuable information to respond with to the customer.[5]

HP's process of complaint ownership has two important aspects to it that affect the customer's relationship with the company. First, the customer is flattered and pleased you have taken the time to listen and act upon whatever wasn't right. Secondly, and perhaps even more important for the future of your relationship, the customer has been made to feel a part of the whole process. In HP's case, the individual customer has been made to feel he or she has played a significant role in shaping how a multibillion dollar company operates. That is positive relationship building.

However, not all companies are paying attention to the complaints from their customers—and missing an important new product development opportunity. An Ernst & Young study, in conjunction with the American Quality Foundation, surveyed 116 computer and peripheral companies in the U.S., Canada, Japan, and Germany. The conclusion reported in the article was, "By failing to channel customer complaints into new product development, U.S. computer companies are missing important opportunities to improve their products. What makes this bad news even worse is that German and Japanese execs are far more likely to use criticism as input to product development operations."[6]

Customers feel good when you show an interest in hearing about problems. If it is something you cannot immediately change, then you need to document it, or "park" it. When you park it, you may put it into a newsletter and then reference it in the cover letter to that customer telling the customer you are capturing this kind of information and it helps your future planning.

Above all, it is important you let the customer know the resolution of their complaint. Two things happen when you close the loop. First, when a customer receives a response that says "this is what we did about the problem," the customer will be more willing to complain in the future. It also means, when doing customer surveys, you will receive a higher percentage of responses as the customer knows action will be taken and they will get some form of feedback. This contributes to building a community of customers.

If you put effective quality management programs in place to handle complaints, you will change defectors and potential terrorists into disciples and apostles. Those customers may go out and become your best salespeople.

Developing a Customer-at-Risk Strategy

While you want to encourage customers to complain, you don't want them to complain unless you can solve the complaint. Unresolved complaints can put the customer at risk. TARP developed data that vividly shows the process of risk analysis. Figure 7-6 shows what happens with the complaint process.

Figure 7-6 shows nearly one-third (32 percent) of customers had experienced problems. Of these, only six out of ten (59 percent) complained. Of the ones complaining, 34 percent were satisfied, 45 percent were mollified, and 21 percent were dissatisfied.

The study then asked customers of their intent to repurchase and their intent to recommend or refer the company to others. You can see that customers who have complained and had their complaint satisfied are slightly more likely to repurchase than customers who have not experienced problems.

Based on this, it would make sense to devise a complaint handling strategy that increases complainer satisfaction levels and increases the number of complainers in that sequence.

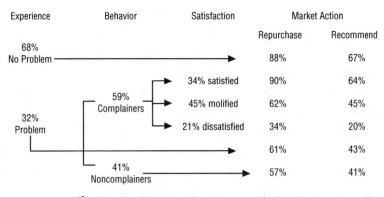

Figure 7-6 Impact of Complaint Handling

Source: Used with permission of TARP.

The 41 percent noncomplainers indicates you will probably lose four out of every ten noncomplainers. The goal then is to increase complaints from those customers who have experienced a problem and to satisfy each complaint. Getting more people to complain without doing a good job of solving problems just causes you to lose more customers.

This leads to TARP's Market-at-Risk calculation, which shows the impact specific problems have on repurchase behavior. The TARP calculation uses the following formula:

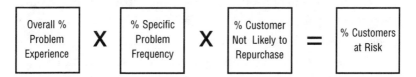

The first step involves surveying customers to determine the level of problem experience. You cannot rely solely on complainers to provide an indication of the number of customers experiencing problems. The best approach is to call the customer shortly following delivery of an order. First, the telemarketing representative thanks the customer for the order and then asks the customer if they experienced any problems with the order process or the product. Most customers are more than willing to relate problem experiences. Next, ask the customer if they will or will not purchase again or offer a referral.

Once you have acquired problem experience information from customers, you can then quantify that information and use the formula to arrive at a customer-at-risk analysis. Figure 7-7 shows this analysis.

This shows 27 percent of those customers with problems had a problem with missed delivery dates. Of those, 10.5 percent indicate they would not repurchase and 52.6 percent indicate they probably would not. This means, for this problem, you are putting between 1.3 percent (45 percent × 27 percent × 10.5 percent) and 6.4 percent (45 percent × 27 percent × 52.5 percent) of customers with late delivery dates at risk. Or, more than 6 percent in this group may become defectors.

On the other hand, this analysis shows those customers experiencing a problem with "product availability within desired time frame," while having a 23 percent frequency, are least likely to defect. This means, when doing planning, you would not concentrate on correcting this problem, but would concentrate your resources on those problems representing higher probabilities of defectors.

This is a resource planning model whose economics can be validated. The information used in the analysis is based on the customer's expected actions. You need to validate this by checking after a period of time to see, if in fact, the customer has defected or continues to buy.

The economic ranking of problems is helpful in securing and allocating funds for solving customer problems. This analysis also allows you to return to this customer irritant after working to reduce defection and actually measure progress through reduced severity of problems.

REACTIVATING DORMANT CUSTOMERS

Another aspect of cultivation is reactivating customers who are no longer buying from you. This can take place as part of the customer cultivation process, or in the acquisition process. A distinction needs to be made between contacting defectors for strategic information and making an effort to regain defectors. Defectors are interviewed to determine the reasons for defection as a means of forestalling having other

Top individual problems		Repurchase			% of customers potentially lost	
Problems experienced (45%)	Problem frequency (%)[1]	Will not[2]	Likely to not[3]		Minimum	Maximum
Meeting promised delivery dates	27	10.5	52.6		1.3	6.4
Product availability within desired time frame	23	0.0	7.7		0.0	0.8
Meeting commitments/follow-through	21	30.0	70.0		2.8	6.6
Equipment/system fixed right the first time	20	22.2	66.7		2.0	6.0
Adequacy of post-sale communications	19	10.0	50.0		0.9	4.3

[1]Based on multiple problem experience
[2]Based on "will not repurchase" only
[3]Based on "will not repurchase" and "might/might not repurchase"

Figure 7-7 Market-at-Risk Estimate

Source: Used with permission of TARP.

valued customers at risk. This process concentrates on the root causes of the defection, not on reactivating the customer.

As was noted previously, customers defect for many reasons. With some reasons, such as going out of business, the customer is not recoverable. However, other types of defectors may be reactivated. For example, if a customer left because of a special competitive price, they may discover the competitor is not meeting all their needs. Or, if a customer left because of a technology or product feature issue, you may have corrected that deficiency and these customers can become prospects.

The communication content, or message, used in a reactivation program depends upon which customer needs were previously not satisfied. As an example, consider the case of defectors who were dissatisfied with a spare parts policy. They needed spare parts delivered within twenty-four hours and did not expect to pay for shipping costs. Now, since their defection, the spare parts policy has changed to twelve hours. The approach in this case would be to send a mailing to each of the defectors and then follow up with a telephone call. The mailing alerts the customer of the change and the phone call enables you to further reinforce your interest in having them return to the customer community.

MEASURING AND MONITORING CULTIVATION STRATEGIES

A key to cultivation is measuring customer attitudes and behaviors on a regular basis. The customer survey is an analytical tool that allows you to understand the successful delivery of external service values to the customer. The development of strategies to deliver those external service values, based on that analysis, drives the organizational structure or the workplace environment, the internal service value, and the implementation of new programs inside your company. Customer surveys give you insight into customer attitudes.

These customer surveys are not the typical customer satisfaction survey. Rather, these behavioral satisfaction surveys measure willingness to repurchase and to refer your product or service.

One aspect of business-to-business marketing that makes customer surveys practical is the size of the market. For example, in consumer markets, customer populations can easily reach the hundreds of thousands or millions. Whereas, in business-to-business markets, some companies may have a total customer base of less than a thousand, with some market segments of fewer than fifty customers. This makes business customer surveys more valuable because they can track a higher percentage of customer's actual behavior, not projected group results. Collecting, recording, and responding to surveys at the individual level adds a new dimension to your business relationship.

One reason companies use customer satisfaction measurements is to verify they are meeting their own standards of performance. For example, Federal Express's standard of delivering packages by 10:30 A.M. and Kraft's standard of filling 100 percent of a grocer's order are based on the assumption that meeting these standards leads to higher customer satisfaction.[7]

Pitfalls of Customer Satisfaction Surveys

Most customer satisfaction surveys provide inappropriate measurements from which to determine customer satisfaction and loyalty. If you recall, the key measurements of customer satisfaction and loyalty are recency, frequency, amount, and referrals. These are the key indicators of customer loyalty. A survey that measures how much the customer "likes" your products or the competition does little to measure a customer's intended buying behavior. You are not interested in how the customer thinks they feel about you, but how satisfied or dissatisfied the customer is with the relationship and the transactions that comprise the relationship. The bottom line for satisfaction is their willingness to buy again and give you referrals.

It is a well-documented fact, however, that customers who indicate they are satisfied still defect. Michael Lowenstein, director of customer-related research at Total Quality Group of Arbor, Inc., commented on this when he noted "surveys show that defectors are just as satisfied with products and services as loyal customers. That's because satisfaction is a rather passive state (check your dictionary definition), requiring a much lower level of involvement than loyalty."[8]

SURVEY DESIGN AND DELIVERY

The design of customer surveys should be handled with care. Warren Hayslip, president of Priority Metrics Group, Inc., identified six common problems with business surveys. These include:[9]

1. *Sloppy introductions.* The survey should not be unprofessional or below the quality of the ongoing relationship. Remember, the survey should be another value-based communication.

2. *Never-ending interview.* Don't tell the customer the survey

will take a few minutes of their time and then spend 40 minutes interrogating the customer.

3. *Misapplied statistics.* As was noted earlier, not all customers are equal and the same applies to surveys. You should have a means of weighting survey responses to take into account key, or AA-graded, customer responses. Their responses are more significant than a D-graded customer. Another misleading aspect of surveys involves overreliance on gross statistics. Hayslip recounted reviewing one manufacturer's program in which they claimed "excellent" results with a 95 percent confidence level. Yet, the survey results were based on a 30 percent return with no response from many of the company's best customers.

4. *Stuck on the aggregate.* While results may be used as index numbers to judge satisfaction, Hayslip warned that suppliers need to go beyond these aggregate calculations and understand the components.

5. *Solutions without value.* Ultimately surveys must be used to create economic value for customers and suppliers alike. If the changes brought on by survey results do not create economic value in the relationship, they should be abandoned.

6. *The broken record.* A survey-based measurement program must have flexibility. Hayslip noted many companies want to use survey data to measure progress over time. Therefore, they require data that is consistent and comparable. Some companies even base bonuses on performance improvements. However, this approach causes these companies to ignore survey modifications or enhancements as they are reluctant to change the survey process.

Survey Guidelines

Building a customer community requires a continual flow of customer feedback. You need to continuously validate that the external service values that cause customer purchasing are still important. You need to reaffirm you are delivering value at every contact point. And, you need to look for ways to continuously improve the offering and the process. Six guidelines for survey design and usage include:

1. Conduct Real-Time Surveys

Surveys should be done on a "real-time" basis. For example, Toshiba sends a postcard survey out after every tenth customer service call. This is a continual process based on contacts. Experience shows you can also continuously survey samples of the market.

2. Avoid Anonymous Surveys of Current Customers

Sometimes companies are reluctant to identify themselves to customers as the entity conducting a survey and use external research firms to conduct the research anonymously. They are fearful the survey is intrusive and will create negative reactions from the customer or the customer's response will be less "truthful" if tied to your company. This attitude, in itself, is a red flag. If you do not have an open dialogue with the customer that enables you to openly engage in customer feedback, then you had better examine your internal attitudes and rebuild them within the company.

Identifying the survey sponsor is supported by Theresa Flanagan and Joan Fredericks, both senior executives with the Quality Management Division of Total Research Corporation. They identified the following advantages that accrue by identifying the sponsor:

- Goodwill is created when you talk to your customers.

- You cannot contact respondents about their answers unless the sponsor's identity is divulged. This ethical guideline is a standard in the market-research industry. Companies may want to follow up with customers, especially when the company has small numbers of customers who create large amounts of revenue.

- Sponsor identification boosts the response rate. Why is a high response rate important? People who respond to surveys can be different from people who do not. Typically, those who do not respond are either considerably more or less dissatisfied. When the identity of the sponsor is revealed, a survey tends to draw additional people who might not otherwise respond, thereby making the findings a better reflection of customer attitudes.[10]

Business-to-business customers do not find surveys intrusive if they are focused on collecting information to deliver value and if they can see feedback or evidence of action. Rather, they appreciate the fact you care enough to solicit their comments and act on their feedback. This appreciation, by the way, is short-lived if you do not act on their feedback. Imagine the positive impact of responding to an individual with action taken from their suggestion.

The preferred method to conduct surveys is through the telephone. That way the person conducting the survey can probe for additional information. For example, a typical telephone survey may begin, "Sally, you're a valued customer of ours and we're talking with our customers to learn more about them and see how we can better work with you." With this type of opening, you are starting a dialogue with Sally and can then move on to the questions in the survey. And, as you get responses, these attributes should be added to the database file for Sally.

3. Use Transaction-Based Surveys

Transaction-based surveys more closely link survey results to an individual. The sooner after the customer has had a transaction with you, the more responsive and personal they are in the survey process. If you are talking with a customer with whom you have not had any transactions during the past three months, their response may be based on vague feelings and multiple contacts. Whereas, if you talk to a customer who spoke with a telemarketer, placed an order, or called about a delivery problem within the past week or ten days, the recollection of the service experience is still fresh. A fax survey immediately following a phone contact can gather very crisp feedback.

4. Ask Customers Directly About Problems

You start by asking customers if they had a problem, did they tell someone about the problem, and what was the outcome. Then you can check to see if there is actually a recorded complaint and what the response was. Through this you can gain insight into how your organization handles complaints. You need access to all customer contact information to manage this type of feedback. If the customer has complained to you, they will expect you to know about it.

5. Give Customers Feedback

It is important to let the customer know what is happening with their input and to provide them with a response. For example, Tandem Computers, for years, has done surveys of every location in their installed base and put the detailed information into their customer database.

Hewlett-Packard pays attention to customer feedback and takes actions based on customer suggestions. Their customer satisfaction survey is contained in an 11-page book that asks more than 100 questions. They also conduct focus groups. HP credits customer feedback as the impetus to become the first computer maker to move their system documentation from paper to CD-ROM. Customer feedback showed customers were unhappy with the documentation, which was 600 lbs. of paper for a midrange computer. They also learned the customers considered documentation important and keeping track of updates was a problem.

The results of this decision were encouraging. Dataquest Inc.'s customer satisfaction survey for minicomputer suppliers showed HP doubling the spread between its score for documentation and the industry average between 1988 and 1989. A follow-up HP survey revealed nearly 50 percent of customers said the CD-ROM service saved up to five hours of systems-management time a month.[11]

6. Use Surveys to Identify Customers at Risk

One way to measure and monitor customers at risk is to track the occurrence of problems by category, such as late shipments, damaged goods, etc. Then survey those customers and ask them behaviorally whether they will continue to buy from you or refer you. You can then link that to the customer and the problem. In six months, you can go back and validate if the customer did in fact buy again.

With this type of survey, you may want to survey behaviors based on external service values. This gives you the opportunity to validate your external service values. For example, if you ask your best customers how you can increase business with them by 15 percent and they respond with things not in your external service values, then you may have to go back and readjust your external service values.

Sample Survey

Resellers and dealers can measure customer loyalty using a survey questionnaire like that shown in Figure 7-8. The survey is conducted using the telephone with the customer service representative provided with a call guide outlining the activities.

You can do a number of analyses with the information you obtain. For example, one approach is to identify reseller loyalty segments. This enables you to classify customers and use those classifications in planning reseller support programs. The segments are:

- *Secure Resellers*

    - Very satisfied with XYZ service and support.

    - Definitely would recommend XYZ Company over competing brands.

    - XYZ's share of business to at least moderately increase during the next year of doing business.

- *Complacent Resellers*

  - Somewhat satisfied with XYZ Company service and support.

  - Probably would recommend XYZ Company over competing brands.

  - XYZ's share of business to remain the same during the next year of doing business.

- *At-Risk Resellers*

  - Neither satisfied nor dissatisfied with XYZ service and support.

  - Might or might not recommend XYZ over competing brands.

  - At best, XYZ's share of business to remain the same during the next year of doing business.

- *Defector Resellers*

  - At best, neither satisfied nor dissatisfied with XYZ service and support.

  - At best, would probably not recommend XYZ over competing brands.

  - At best, XYZ's share of business to moderately decrease during the next year of doing business.

Introductions:

Introduction to include:
- Calling on behalf of XYZ Company
- Identify decision maker if not already known
- Calling to better understand the key drivers of satisfaction and loyalty

Questions:

Only closed-ended questions should be prompted.

1. Overall, how satisfied are you with your relationship with XYZ Company?

   5. Very satisfied
   4. Somewhat satisfied
   3. Neither satisfied nor dissatisfied (neutral)
   2. Somewhat dissatisfied
   1. Very dissatisfied
   0. Do not know/Not applicable

2. Overall, how satisfied are you with the (product category) service and support that you receive from XYZ Company?

   5. Very satisfied
   4. Somewhat satisfied
   3. Neither satisfied nor dissatisfied (neutral)
   2. Somewhat dissatisfied
   1. Very dissatisfied
   0. Do not know/Not applicable

3. Have you experienced any significant service and support related problems with XYZ Company in the last year?

   2. Yes (Go to question #4)
   1. No (Go to question #7)

4. Could you describe the most significant service or support related problems that you experienced?

5. Did you inform XYZ Company of this problem?

6. How satisfied were you with XYZ Company's ability to resolve your problem?

5. Very satisfied
4. Somewhat satisfied
3. Neither satisfied nor dissatisfied (neutral)
2. Somewhat dissatisfied
1. Very dissatisfied
0. Do not know/Not applicable

7. How likely are you to recommend XYZ Company product(s) over competing brands? Would you say . . . .

   5. Definitely would
   4. Probably would
   3. Might or might not
   2. Probably would not
   1. Definitely would not
   0. Do not know/Not applicable

8. Please estimate what percentage of your total product sales in this product category come from XYZ Company products.

9. Considering your next business year, will XYZ Company's share of this product category most likely . . .

   5. Significantly increase
   4. Moderately increase
   3. Remain the same
   2. Moderately decrease
   1. Significantly decrease
   0. Do not know/Not applicable

10. What are the specific factors that differentiate XYZ Company's products from other manufacturers of the same products and promote you to continue to do business with XYZ Company?

11. What is the largest barrier that you have in doing business with XYZ Company?

12. What additional services and support would you like to see from XYZ Company that they currently do not provide?

Figure 7-8 Sample Survey Questionnaire: Reseller/Dealer Call Guide

This process of cultivating the customer requires diligence and sensitivity. Five aspects of the cultivation process need repeating.

- First, this has to be a disciplined process in which you follow the contact plan derived from customer information.

- Second, you need to develop a harvesting or penetration approach that leverages your existing customer relationships.

- Third, you need to listen to the voice of the customer. You need to be sensitive to what the customer is saying at every point of contact.

- Fourth, you not only have to listen to the customer, you need to take action and let the customer know you are taking action.

- Fifth, you need to review your customer database and identify dormant customers, then look for a means to reactivate them.

- Finally, you need to monitor the process as a means of continuous improvement. Monitoring the process enables you to validate external service values, respond to new customer needs, and detect customers-at-risk.

COMMUNITY BUILDING IN ACTION: BUSINESSFORMS

Account management for the BusinessForms division involves all the processes discussed in previous chapters. This includes a customer contact plan that integrates mail, phone, and field contacts. As the division follows the plan, several additional activities are required in the customer retention process. First, they need to know who is a customer. In other words, they have a list of dentists with at least a $400,000 practice who have purchased from them in the past. Now they need a means to identify which customers are active, which are not, and which may be at risk.

After reviewing the customer transaction histories in the database, the division determined an active customer is one who has purchased a minimum of $1,000 in forms in the past twelve months and purchases forms at least once every three months. Each buyer was reviewed for additional types of forms and dentists in other offices were also targeted for testimonials.

Next, they reviewed the database information and identified those customers who have purchased from them in the past but do not meet the criteria for an active customer. These customers are then targeted for reactivation, which is a process used as part of the acquisition phase of community building (Chapter 8).

The division next identified those customers who may be at risk. That is, those customers who may have stopped buying from them. The division wants to identify these customers *before* they defect.

The approach the division used was, if the dentist had not placed an order within the past two months, they sent a postcard reminding the dentist to check his or her forms inventory. If no order is received within ten days, they call the dentist as a further reminder and also to determine if the dentist has a problem. If the dentist has purchased less than

$1,000 in the past ten months, they check for product lines that may not have been purchased and then call to survey for potential problems.

Using this type of early warning system enables the division to identify potential problems in the relationship before the dentist makes the decision to defect.

As part of the account management process, the Business-Forms division also monitors the customer relationship through customer surveys. One technique they use is to send a survey to a dentist following the shipment of every third order or once every six months. If the survey is not returned within ten days, a telephone follow-up is used to obtain the survey information. Through this method, the division can continually monitor the needs of the dentist and identify problem areas before they become serious.

Next, BusinessForms looked at the data to see what specific types of problems exist and how severe are the problems. They found the most severe problem is custom form order delays resulting in orders not arriving on time. They found 10 percent of customer problems included in this area, with 60 percent of those with the problem stating they would not buy again. They also found, when analyzing the data, 20 percent of their customers had some problem.

When they applied the customer-at-risk analysis to this data, they found they were putting 1.2 percent of their customers at risk (20 percent × 10 percent × 60 percent). They also know the expected lifetime value of a customer is $8,300 and the expected value of a lost customer is $5,000. With 20,000 active customers, this means custom forms arriving late puts 240 customers at risk (20,000 × 1.2 percent) at a loss of $1,200,000 (240 × $5,000).

With this type of hard economic data, the BusinessForms division can now justify investing in improving the custom forms process.

Notes

1. Joan Koob Cannie, *Turning Lost Customers into Gold: . . . and the Art of Achieving Zero Defections* (New York: Amacon, 1994), 11.

2. Claes Fornell and Birger Wernerfelt, "Defensive Marketing Strategy by Customer Complaint Management: A Theoretical Analysis," *Journal of Marketing Research,* November 1987, 338–339.

3. William H. Davidow and Bro Uttal, *Total Customer Service: The Ultimate Weapon* (New York: Harper & Row, 1989), 15.

4. John Goodman, Scott M. Broetzmann, and Dianne S. Ward, "Preventing TQM Problems: Measured Steps Toward Customer-Driven Quality Improvement," *National Productivity Review,* Autumn 1993, 557–558.

5. Terence P. Pare, "How to Find Out What They Want," *Fortune,* Autumn/Winter 1993, 40.

6. Rick Whiting, "Customer Complaints Are an Untapped Source for Product Ideas, *Electronic Business,* July 1992, 7.

7. Davidow and Uttal, 196–197.

8. Michael W. Lowenstein, "The Voice of the Customer," *Small Business Reports,* December 1993, 58.

9. Warren Hayslip, "Measuring Customer Satisfaction in Business Markets," *Quality Progress,* April 1994, 85–86.

10. Theresa A. Flanagan and Joan O. Fredericks, "Improving Company Performance Through Customer-Satisfaction Measurement and Management," *National Productivity Review,* Spring 1993, 248.

11. Jack Shandle, "Learning How to Listen," *Electronics,* May 1991, 49.

8

ACQUIRING NEW CUSTOMERS

Acquiring new customers represents a major investment for any company. A rule-of-thumb, which is well documented, is it costs five to ten times more (sometimes more than twenty times) to acquire new customers than it does to retain an existing one. That is, to get $1,000 of revenue from a new customer may cost you five or ten or twenty times more than from an existing customer. The goal is to develop an acquisition strategy that makes maximum use of dollars and produces a reasonable return on investment. Return is revenue and profits over the customer's life, not the revenue from the first purchase. Therefore, customer acquisition is a natural extension of customer cultivation.

In acquiring new customers, nonproductive cold calling, which seems so prevalent among business-to-business marketers, is replaced with a systematic approach for generating qualified leads based on the segments and value-based contacts refined during customer cultivation. You want to eliminate calling on unqualified leads generated through advertising or some other medium. Rather, leads are prequalified before being sent to the sales channel. The message content is the same value-based message that has been documented by working with your best customers—segment by segment.

Economically acquiring new customers is possible only through knowledge of current customers. This involves developing an acquisition strategy based on a process using targeting, segmentation, grading of accounts, value-based contacts, and purchasing processes—the same as used for building customer loyalty.

The Integrated Marketing Model (Figure 8-1) shows the acquisition process in the upper portion of the model.

In the model, acquisition differs from other aspects of the community process as it does not focus on building a relationship, rather it focuses on an event. That event is to get a potential customer to raise his or her hand—to indicate they have an interest in your product or service. Then the sales process can be advanced until it results in a purchase. *The challenge is to get the (economically) right people to hold up their hands and then convert them into loyal customers.*

EXISTING CUSTOMERS DEFINE NEW CUSTOMERS

While current customers are the best source of growth through referrals as well as product and account penetration, they are valuable for another reason: They are the base from which you build the acquisition strategy. They help you define the "target" in target marketing and the "segments" of segmentation.

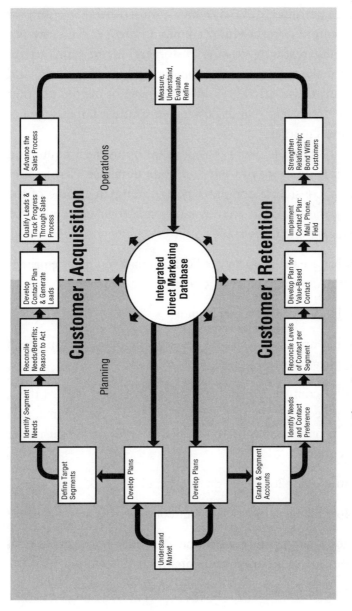

Figure 8-1 Integrated Marketing Model

© Hunter Business Direct, Inc. Developed by J. M. McIntyre.

Your customer database has a substantial amount of attribute information useful for building prospective customer profiles. You research existing customers, identify the attributes that make these customers unique and individualistic, and then group those attributes into clusters, or segments, that have common needs. These clusters constitute a target segment of your total market.

The ability to segment is dependent upon the amount and type of information you have in your database. To demonstrate this, consider a computer printer company. Some of the questions the company may want to ask their customers for segmentation purposes are:

- What are the primary applications that you use the printer for? Are any unique to our printer and why?

- Why did you buy our printer?

- What are the functional titles of the people within each application?

- Who controls the purse strings? In effect, who is the key decision maker for printers? If we get a name, add it to our database—this is penetration of the customer location.

- How many locations do you have?

- How many employees in your company? At your location?

- How many printers do you currently have installed at your location? In your company?

- How fast are you growing?

- Are you expanding your computerization of work?

- How much do you spend on toner? On ink jet fluid?

By asking customers focused questions, you compile a list of key attributes for developing target segments for customer acquisition. When you take the next step, of identifying attributes that will comprise a target segment, you should focus only on those needed to select segments, specify needs, and define purchasing roles.

IDENTIFYING SEGMENT NEEDS

Once you segmented your existing customer base, you then validated the needs associated with each segment. You documented these needs in the customer database. You conducted the needs assessment, which also identified the external service values that drive buying behavior. Now, you take the same information and apply it to a target market. For example, if a segment of your current customer base values toll-free technical support and overnight delivery, then other individuals with the same attributes and applications of that target segment should value these same services.

Using your database, you access "selectable attributes," which identify individuals around business applications and common sets of needs. The major grouping is the target market and the subgroups are the segments. Figure 8-2 shows a sample profile:

The first column in Figure 8-2 is a summary of the attributes for a market, in this case, manufacturing. The next column summarizes the attributes of the best customers in the

manufacturing target market. Then, the next two columns
are summaries of two prospect lists that are available, either
as a mailing list or as a media profile.

When you take this approach, you look for prospects that
fit the profile of your best customers. When you find prospects
that look like your best customers, they should have the same
set of needs. This takes some of the guesswork out of new
business acquisition.

Attributes	Installed Base	Best Accounts	Target Market 1	Target Market 2
1. SICs	Mfg. (20-40)	Chemical	Petroleum	Rubber Products
2. # of employees	500–6,000	5,000+	1,000–2,500	1,000–10,000
3. # of plants	1–10	5+	5+	1–10
4. # of units produced/hour	100–350/min	250/min	100/min	250/min
5. # of production lines	1–10 lines	5-10+ lines	3+ lines	1–3 lines
6. Annual Sales	$10–500 million	Fortune 500	$200 million –Fortune 500	$100 million

Figure 8-2 Segment Attribute Profile

TARGETING THE "RIGHT" CUSTOMERS

As you go through the process of segmenting and targeting
customers, you need to be aware that not every customer is
best for you. You need to determine which are the "right"
customers to pursue. This is a fundamental requirement when
building a community of customers. Within any community,

whether civic, religious, or professional, there exists a single-ness of purpose or a fundamental commonality. While diversity is part of community, new customers must fit into the community; they must have the same needs and buying behaviors as other members of the customer community.

Bain & Company's loyalty management director, Frederick Reichheld, stresses targeting the right type of customers. He stated, "Customers are obviously an essential ingredient of a loyalty-based system, and success depends on their staying with the company a long time. But not all customers are equal. Companies should target the 'right' customers—not necessarily the easiest to attract or the most profitable in the short term but those who are likely to do business with the company over time. For various reasons, some customers don't ever stay loyal to one company, no matter what value they receive. The challenge is to avoid as many of these people as possible in favor of customers whose loyalty can be developed."[1]

ACQUISITION PLANNING

After segmenting your customers into target markets and segments, you use that information in the acquisition planning process. You now want to combine the needs analysis, external service values, and value-added communications into a plan. This is similar to the process used to construct the Customer Contact Plan in Chapter 4.

In effect, you are replicating the processes you went through when determining the value-based contacts and determining how, when, and about what your existing customers wanted you to contact them. Now, the focus shifts from building relationships to getting a prospect to show interest, i.e., respond in some manner to the offer.

Competitive Positioning

One of the tools used in refining acquisition plans is the competitive analysis used in Chapter 3. In a competitive positioning analysis, you need to take into account the unfulfilled needs, as defined by current customers in that target segment.

How you segment can make a difference in positioning. For example, DuPont found, in the medical X-ray market, traditional demographic segmentation did not give them adequate information. Prior to 1984, DuPont considered only two segments in this market, federal government and all other hospitals. But, the market was changing with the emergence of buying groups, multihospital chains, and nonhospital health care delivery systems. So DuPont needed to resegment their market.

DuPont's study found, as the company had presumed, institutions with different buying behaviors could be segmented on the type of institution and the responsibilities of those influencing and making decisions. As a result, the company identified three market segments. These included:

1. Groups specifying a single supplier that must be used by all member hospitals, such as investor-owned hospital chains;

2. Groups selecting a small number of suppliers from which individual hospitals may select needed products; and

3. A private group practice and nonhospital segment.

As Gary Coles and James Culley, DuPont research analysts, noted, "Our revised segmentation strategy allowed us to focus our resources—particularly our highly trained field salespeople—on the decision-making dynamics of each segment."[2]

Determining the "Offer"

Once you have analyzed unfulfilled needs and product features, compared product or service offerings with the competition, developed a competitive position, and defined key benefits and unique benefits, the next step is the offer. Bob Stone, the widely respected direct marketing authority, said the offer, or proposition, you make to customers "can mean the difference between success and failure."[3] The advantage this acquisition strategy has is it is based on *unique benefits that have been defined by your customers.*

Remember, the customer's basic needs are what you need to satisfy to be in the market segment. *Unfulfilled needs are market opportunities.* So, when looking at a target market, you need to ask what kind of unfulfilled needs exist in the target market that you are satisfying with your current customers. Don't be concerned with future needs—those things you're going to develop in the future—when developing an acquisition plan, although these can be helpful for strategic planning. You want to focus on unfulfilled needs, which are really an opportunity to differentiate and provide a solution.

If you then group together those people who have common sets of unfulfilled needs, you can create "test cells" and then go to those cells with a message, which becomes your offer. The offer is then communicated through a contact medium, which could include advertising, electronic media, direct mail, telemarketing, and field sales. These media are integrated and synergistic because they come out of a process beginning with the same definition of needs and unique benefits for this segment.

Developing a Value-Added Communication Plan

One of the first considerations in developing a value-added communication plan is an economic one. You need to analyze target segments in terms of expected lifetime value, acquisition cost, and customer fit. Until you know what you can expect from the target segment, you cannot determine how much to invest in acquisition.

An example helps illustrate this. Assume you are selling modular office desks and accessories, such as credenzas and cabinets. One target segment is light manufacturing. The database shows the characteristics of your most profitable customers in this segment include companies with facilities between 15,000 and 50,000 square feet and an employee count of between 30 and 150. It also shows, over a five-year period, the customer will return $2,700 in profits. Based on this, and assuming you want to show a profit, you determine you can invest 50 percent of the anticipated five-year profits from a new customer into acquiring that customer. Therefore, you would be willing to invest $1,350 to gain a new customer.

This gives a starting point in building a communication plan. You next develop an acquisition budget for this target segment. The goal often is to identify and qualify a prospect so a field salesperson can make a single face-to-face contact to close the first sale (or at least some minimal contact).

In the case of the office desk manufacturer, assume a field

sales contact costs $150 and the field salesperson closes one in every three calls. This means the cost to close a qualified prospect is $450. Based on previous experience, the company knows it can convert qualified leads one-third of the time. That is, once a prospect raises his or her hand, or responds to a communication message, it knows 33 percent of the qualified leads will be converted to a first-time sale. Based on this, you can take the remaining $900 from the $1,350 budget and spend approximately $300 per each qualified lead ($900 × 33 percent).

Next the company determines how many generated leads become qualified leads. For this example, let's assume 25 percent of those who hold up their hands become qualified leads. This means they can spend $75 per lead if they want to attract new customers profitably. If it costs $25 to qualify a lead, then the cost of a new lead cannot exceed $50. Figure 8-3 summarizes this analysis.

Estimated lifetime profit per customer	$ 2,700
50% profit retention	1,350
Per customer acquisition budget	$ 1,350
Field sales cost (three contacts per sale)	450
	$ 900
Qualified prospect closure	x 0.33
Cost per qualified lead	$ 300
Ratio of qualified vs. unqualified leads	x 0.25
Cost per prospect lead	$ 75
Qualifying cost	$ 25
Cost per new lead	$ 50

Figure 8-3 New-Lead Budget Analysis

With this information, they can now develop a contact plan based on an affordable cost, reconciled with the preferred method of contact for new product. The preferred method of contact is based on projecting current customers' preferences onto the target segment.

When this type of economic analysis is complete, you have performance measurements to use in evaluating the effectiveness of lead generation programs. A point that should be stressed is you always start from the "best" programs and move to more marginal ones. If you can't make the best programs work, don't bother testing beyond that.

Avoid Selling New Products to New Customers

One of the more fallacious marketing approaches is developing new products for the purpose of entering new markets. This may be necessary for a start-up company without an existing customer base. But, it is risky, expensive, and dangerous for established companies. The big problem is that a new customer acquired with new products seldom looks like or economically behaves like your current customers.

This is supported by PIMS research (Figure 8-4), which shows the probability of success in offering new products to existing customers is about ten times higher than that for new customers.

	Old Products	New Products/Services
Established Customers	95%	50%
New Customers	25%	5%

Figure 8-4 Probability of Success

INTEGRATING CONTACT MEDIA

Since acquiring new customers is a difficult and costly process, you need to take full advantage of what each media type offers. The media types typically used in acquisition are:

- *Space advertising*—Advertising, which can include industry trade publications, directory listings, yellow pages, card decks, etc., is a low-cost-per-contact medium.

- *Broadcast advertising*—While not widely used in business-to-business marketing, it can prove effective for regional or local area promotions. However, some companies, notably Federal Express, have been successful with broadcast advertising as a business-to-business marketing tool.

- *PR/Publicity*—While PR and publicity activities are the lowest cost per contact, they are less effective than advertising as the sender does not control the message, the media, or the timing of the message. Typical activities include press releases, new product introductions, literature and sales brochure releases, customer testimonials, and other types of editorial material.

- *Electronic media*—The traditional electronic media include e-mail, broadcast fax, and fax-on-demand. The Internet and World Wide Web hold promise for new and focused low-cost contact.

- *Direct mail*—Direct mail offers many choices in formats and delivery types. These can include solo direct mail pieces, co-op postcard decks, co-op package inserts, package inserts, customer newsletters, and similar communication.

- *Telemarketing*—Telemarketing is used for prospecting, profiling, customer service, and technical assistance.

- *Face-to-face*—In the acquisition process, face-to-face is effective at trade shows and other types of industry gatherings, speeches, and seminars.

Two contact types that are quickly emerging—alliances and electronic media—require special attention. Alliances involve establishing relationships with other service or product suppliers that your customer uses that will benefit both parties. For example, shared leads, shared exhibit space, and shared customer databases are areas of significant economic value.

Electronic media has received much attention. For example, in 1990 only about 1,000 commercial enterprises had a presence on the Internet. In early 1996, estimates had more than 25,000 companies on the World Wide Web with more than 500 being added each week.[4] Many companies are experimenting with and using their presence on electronic bulletin boards and on-line services to acquire new customers.

While media channels such as the Internet and on-line services offer a unique communication approach, they lack the ability to direct a message at a target audience. In fact, they invite people to "visit" them. The inquirer or visitor must access the information, i.e., they have to find you. At present, little control exists over matching the message uniquely to the inquirer. Your task is to look attractive to a unique set of "potential" customers.

If the acquisition goal is to target prospects that look like your best current customers, electronic channels often fall short, at this time. Targeting comes from self-profiling by the inquirer and prompting to the electronic channel from other media; that is, referencing a home page in targeted mailings, fax, or phone conversations. The Internet will certainly continue to grow in functionality and value as a source of new leads.

Probably the most effective use of the Internet is to make product information accessible to customers. For example, GE Plastics, a $5 billion subsidiary of General Electric, has more than 1,500 pages of information on 11 resin product lines available to customers through the Internet's World Wide Web. This includes technical data, application notes, and specifications. To encourage customers to access this information, the company offers customers a customized version of Internet access software.[5]

However, making product information available upon demand, while providing a convenient service to the customer, should not replace any of the elements of the customer contact plan. Synchronized and planned contacts are the cornerstone of building a customer community.

Evaluating Contact Media

Two major criteria are used when evaluating contact media—efficiency and effectiveness. Efficiency relates to the cost per contact of the medium or communications channel. You want to use the least costly method to deliver the message to the customer. Effectiveness relates to how the customer prefers to receive this type of information; that is, which medium or communication channel will be most successful in having the prospect pay attention to the message. You need to balance efficiency and effectiveness for an integrated contact plan to be economically justifiable.

For example, face-to-face is the most effective medium or channel to have the prospect understand the content of a message. In face-to-face, a dialogue develops and both participants have the advantage of nonverbal communication signals for feedback. However, face-to-face is the least cost-efficient channel. Therefore, you want to leverage this high cost with lower-cost media. This is balancing efficiency and effectiveness.

One of the most cost-efficient media for lead generation is business-to-business magazines, or trade publications. A Cahners Publishing study showed 96 out of 100 buyers of industrial products read trade publications. The major attraction for trade advertising is most publications use reader service cards, which are a convenient direct response device an interested reader can use to request further information about an advertised product. Some publishers are using 800 numbers for "hot prospects" who want immediate information and some offer fax-back services for the same purpose. For the advertiser, the publication provides them with periodic reports containing a list of all those who responded to the advertisement. The detail of these reports varies from publisher to publisher, but some can even provide an analysis of which respondents also requested competitive information.[6]

For the most part, however, the time lag in getting these leads from the publisher makes their value decline significantly and often the inquirer cannot recall the request for information. That's why an 800 number is critical for quick response. This also lets you acquire additional qualification information during the initial contact with the inquirer. It is also less expensive for an inquirer to contact you than for you to call someone on the phone.

According to Cahners, half of all reader service card respondents are curious because they are trying to solve a specific problem, and the other half are interested to keep current on ways to solve potential problems. Another group of studies showed one-eighth of all inquiries lead to a sale, five-eighths were from potential purchasers, and one-fourth bought the product from someone else. [7]

One of the ironies of business-to-business media advertising is that companies, usually management, have a fixation with four-color advertising. This is the most expensive form of advertising and its impact (i.e., effectiveness) often does not justify the cost when measuring value in cost per qualified lead. For example, some management metrics use awareness and recall as principal criteria. These are "soft measures" when related to new business revenue. A better measure, yet still short of the cost of qualified lead, is "considerations" where the value of lead generation is calculated based on cost per opportunity to present or demonstrate the product or service.

If you must do awareness advertising, then simply set up two advertising budgets—one for awareness and the other for qualified lead generation. Measure each appropriately. However, be cautious, as some companies are now finding, the better their lead generation campaigns become, the more they outscore awareness campaigns on awareness measurements.

The goal is to optimize the lead generation process. You can do that, when evaluated on the cost per qualified lead, through black and white, application-based, fractional-page ads in vertical publications that reach target segments. In effect, the message is far more effective than the form of the ad. Because the message is built around external service values, it should appeal to those target segments that look like your current customer segment.

An advertising medium mostly overlooked is the card deck. These are typically 3″ × 5″ cards wrapped in cellophane and sent to the subscribers of a magazine. Many consider this to be equivalent to consumer "junk mail." However, card decks can be effective and they are the most efficient mail contact medium. Card decks will cost only $0.01–0.02 per contact. You get the information directly and not filtered through a magazine. Your audience is the same as the sponsoring magazine's. While card decks do generate a certain number of "literature collectors," this can be an extremely low-cost method of generating leads that, when qualified, still come within a budget. Remember, when analyzing media, you need to generate qualified leads within the constraints of a predetermined budget, which is based on an expected return on your acquisition investment.

Another consideration in the media selection process is to consider the time required for planning, creative, and execution for each media type. For example, a direct mail program may actually take 15 weeks from inception through mailing. If you're doing telemarketing planning, you have to sit down and review the plans and try to understand the economics of the plan before you begin calling. The fact that you have a telemarketing center set up doesn't mean you can economically afford, for example, to call 11,000 sheet metal fabricators. You have to evaluate the economics before you begin calling and possibly narrow the universe with mail contact or some other profiling tool.

Designing a Contact Plan

In the acquisition planning process, you build a customer contact plan similar to the one developed for current customers (Chapter 4). However, in this case, you do not have information on customer contact preferences since you have not had contact with the prospects. Therefore, you project onto the prospects the same preferences of your current customers within each segment. Experience has shown this is a realistic approach.

List and Media Selection

One area that can cause difficulty is matching the attributes of the target segment with the circulation profile of a magazine or the selects available from a direct mail list. That is one reason that testing is required. With an advertisement, test it with the most likely publication that delivers readers similar to your target segment. With a direct mail list, you would select the list that best matches the attributes of your target segment and then mail to a sample of that list.

In any test situation, you should target your best prospects first. If it won't work with the best then it won't work with anyone. Too often marketers approach this stage of the process *using the reverse approach*—targeting the least likely to raise their hands. Their thinking goes like this: "We don't know what we're talking about, so we start with people who, if we don't do it right, won't hurt us." This means you'll never get it right.

Another mistake is to test each of a number of target segments without picking the best segment in each market. The same problem occurs. If it doesn't work you still don't know if some segment might work. What you are doing is going after the best prospect, finding out what they want, and then giving them the best offer you have. If it doesn't work, you're dead. If it does, then you may be able to fine-tune it and have it work for another tier of prospects. And if that works, you can fine-tune it again and it may work for still another tier of prospects.

The importance of testing cannot be overemphasized. Understanding segment attributes, and how to apply them to media selection, is a critical step. Consider this: you have a choice of more than 35,000 mailing lists and more than 12,000 trade publications and business journals reaching more than *five million* companies. Being able to select the names of prospects that best meet your key attributes can make or break an acquisition program.

Captive Market Segments

Captive market segments present some unique opportunities and difficulties. Captive markets are those market segments that are relatively small in size. This is fairly common in some business-to-business markets, especially with those marketing to original equipment manufacturers. The total universe size in a market segment may be less than 1,000 or even in the low hundreds.

When you have a market segment in which the universe is relatively small, your acquisition plan looks more like a cultivation plan. Since the physical number of individuals you have to reach is manageable and they often have more shared communication among themselves, you can use more personal forms of communication on a more frequent basis, provided they are economically justified.

Cutting into the sheet metal industry. Several examples will help demonstrate the advantages and disadvantages you can encounter with captive markets. In one case, a company had developed a plasma arc torch for a two-dimensional robot arm that cuts sheet metal, which produced significant productivity gains. They truly believed they could dominate the sheet metal fabrication industry.

The universe was small, in the range of 9,500 to 11,000 companies. However, the problem they faced was none of the industry research sources could select which of those fabricators were handling hundreds of thousands of pounds of galvanized steel and which were in someone's basement. Lists of sheet metal fabricators were available, but the selects were not.

Obviously it would not be economically feasible to call 11,000 companies. The solution was to approach the trade publication that reached sheet metal fabricators and suggest a joint project. The company would conduct market research among the subscribers of the magazine, which it would exclusively share with the publisher. In return, the publication would add the category "number of employees" to their annual subscriber survey, since this was a key attribute of larger fabricators. The result was the size of the target universe shrunk to 2,500. Now, the company can develop an economically justified acquisition program.

Many times, an acquisition plan will resemble a cultivation plan. For example, a company in Chicago owns the pipecutting market for any type of pipe over 12″ in diameter.

They have 80 percent of the worldwide market. They know who the other 20 percent are, therefore they would not use an acquisition model in going after the remaining 20 percent, but would use a variation of the cultivation model.

Tapping into vending machines. Another example is a software company that developed a product for the vending machine market. The product appeals to those companies that stock and service vending machines. The company's initial market research showed the best prospects for the software would be companies of a certain size. This size was translated into companies having three or more service trucks. By checking vehicle registration records, the company determined their market for this product was about 1,000 companies.

Assuming the software has been sold to 100 companies, the company now knows the remaining universe of prospects is 900. So, they need to build a relationship with the entire target market. With this type of captive market, they would want to cultivate the 100 current customers for upgrades, referrals, and to sell add-ons. The 900 can be treated almost the same as current customers. If they establish a goal of capturing 50 new customers a year, they can then set up a program similar to an account management program. By knowing current customers' needs, external service values, value-based communication preferences, etc., the company knows how much the 50 new customers will represent in lifetime value and, from that, can establish a budget for acquiring them.

With this information, the company can build a contact model that might include a newsletter, trade show, phone contacts, etc. They can afford to cultivate this captive universe rather than use typical acquisition tools. Where this really works is the business-to-business marketer who can segment markets to such a finite point that every segment is a captive universe. This comes very close to the concept of marketing to a market size of one.

LEAD MANAGEMENT

Once a lead has been generated, that is, someone raises a hand, you need to set into motion a lead management process that qualifies leads, advances the selling process, and measures responses. Figure 8-5 shows this must be a closed loop system.

Lead Qualification

Setting up the database. As leads come in they should be entered into a database with the source of the lead noted. This could range from bingo card responses, bounce-back cards, trade show requests, faxes, etc. At this stage, the lead is considered an "inquiry." Someone is inquiring for more information on your products or services. They may or may not be a qualified prospect. Again, the prospect database uses the individual's name as the key identifier, similar to the customer database. It should also include any additional information, such as street address, etc., provided as part of the response.

It is important to enter the name of the person responding at the earliest possible moment. This becomes a critical part of the measurement and evaluation process. The database chronicles all the company's activities related to customer acquisition and is used to analyze lead sources, level of qualified leads per source, percent of qualified leads, cost per qualified lead, etc.

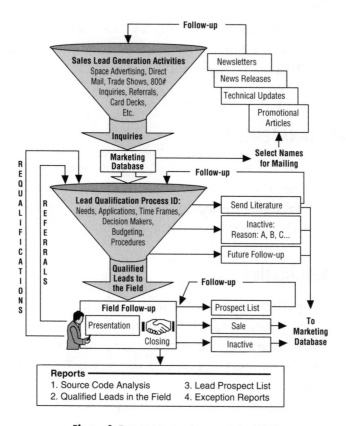

Figure 8-5 Lead Management Model

© Hunter Business Direct, Inc.

Every event in the process, from the advertising activity that generated the lead through direct mail and telephone qualification of leads through the first sale, is captured in the database. It's a powerful tool for relating marketing actions with marketplace results.[8]

Companies many times do not make this effort to chronicle the lead process. They typically cite lack of resources as the reason. Yet, they spend thousands of dollars on advertising activities with little or no understanding of the return on their investment or which marketing programs were effective. As a result, they continue to repeat the activities, many of which are producing low returns.

Once an inquiry is entered in the database, you compare the inquiry with the information already in the database. This helps determine the type and level of response. For example, Dr. Judy Jones may be a professor who asks her students to collect information. This produces similar addresses in the database and you can respond based on that knowledge. Or, the street address for Tom is the same as Pete's, who is already a customer of yours. This tells you someone else at Pete's location has an interest and you would want to follow up on this inquiry with a phone call. Or, you may want to call Pete and get a referral to Tom.

Also look for matches with current key national accounts, with the current installed base, with affiliates of the installed base, and with special segments of the installed base, such as government. If you can identify leads attached to an existing relationship, you can leverage the existing relationship to better qualify the lead.

Responding to leads. Timely lead response is mandatory. The half-life for someone remembering they sent in an inquiry based on a specific need is ten to fourteen days. However, if the lead is tied to an event, such as a trade show, the person will remember it longer.

A recent five-year study measuring fulfillment of reader-response cards showed, on average, only three-quarters of responses sent in by potential customers were followed up by salespeople. Of those that were answered, it took an average of two months for the prospects to receive a phone call or brochure. These results suggest it doesn't matter how much time and money you spend on your marketing if your sales-force isn't getting the leads, or worse, if they're not following up on them. This not only leads to lost sales, it may leave neg-ative impressions in the minds of your potential customers.[9]

Leads you receive through an 800 number or regular tele-phone line should be handled immediately. These represent prime targets for qualification. When that person is calling, they are in a mindset to focus on a problem they perceive your product or service will satisfy. You need to elicit infor-mation from them to qualify the lead, then add it to your database and, at the same time, establish the urgency of their problem. These can quickly turn into "hot" leads you for-ward to the field salesperson for immediate action and you fax or express ship the product information to the caller.

Qualifying leads. Lead qualification is a subject that has been widely discussed and written about. Yet, too often, com-panies get their leads, send the literature package, and forward the lead to the field sales channel. The worst approach is gen-erating leads and sending them direct to the field office or reseller without any means of tracking effectiveness of the lead generation effort. This is the "black hole" or "Bermuda Tri-angle" of lead generation systems. Field salespeople with a desk drawer crammed full of leads, some several years old, are not uncommon.

By qualifying leads, you increase the productivity of the field sales organization. Most salespeople do not have the time to follow up on leads, unless the lead has been determined to be a "hot" prospect, or someone with an immediate buying interest. To avoid the drawer full of old leads, you manage the lead process and only forward leads to the field that have been prequalified to meet predefined field sales criteria.

Some company managements delude themselves in believing that since their reseller group or sales channel partners are on commission, they do not have to qualify leads. The economics tied to optimizing lead generation, the value of information about your customer, and channel accountability demand the management of lead qualification.

The key qualifiers are buying mode and time. You want to know if the person sending an inquiry is a potential buyer and within what time frame. During the call, you also have the opportunity to collect attribute information for inclusion in the database.

You then can grade and quantify leads so the field only receives qualified ones. Those leads with no immediate need, but a future interest, are retained in the database and become targets for a synchronized communication process that maintains contact with them and insures they are informed on developments about their areas of interest. The goal is to advance them along the sales process so that they migrate from "prospect" to potential buyer.

When sending information after the call, include a marketing letter that references the call in the opening and directs the inquirer to the pertinent information in the catalogs and other literature. This enhances the value of the communication with the prospect. It also helps insure the information gets to the prospect. For example, chances are the literature package won't be delayed in the mail room or by a protective administrative assistant if they see it is being sent in response to a specific phone conversation.

Typically, companies will have a standard response package of literature they send to inquiries. This then may be followed by a phone call, or more likely, the lead is sent to the field sales channel involved, such as a field salesperson, distributor, dealer, or sales rep, for follow-up. This is a waste of paper and postage. You should call leads before sending information. For example, seven times out of 10 if you call first you will send information unique to the call. By calling first, you insure you are sending value-based communication to the inquirer, you strengthen the cover letter with a reference to your call, and you have the opportunity to better qualify the prospect.

To test this, start taking new inquiries coming into your office and write down what you would typically send each. Then call the person and qualify the lead, determining what interests they have. Then compare what you will send them to what you originally planned to send them. In most cases, you will change your original response and/or focus on a specific part of the fulfillment package. The key performance measurement for this process is deliverability and retention of requested information.

Advancing the Sales Process

When the lead has been qualified as a prospective, as opposed to immediate, buyer, you need to develop a program that will move them along the sales process. This involves developing a value-based communication plan, similar to the one developed for existing customers. Here, you want to establish a program in which you continue to maintain contact with the prospect through predetermined value-based communication. This typically involves a combination of direct mail, telemarketing, and, in some instances, field sales contacts.

Closing the sale. You advance the sales process with things like demos, quotes, and face-to-face presentations when the customer has indicated a willingness to buy. When the customer makes a purchasing decision, you confirm the close with the customer. You thank the customer and tell them you understand they want you to order this product for them and you'll be shipping it out in "X" days and then you will be calling them back to see how everything works.

With this approach, you are building the expectation that this is a relationship. It's bonding with the customer. It's allowing the customer and you to set the expectation that you are going to move beyond this transaction.

Measuring and Monitoring the Lead Process

The success of an acquisition program is based on the ability to measure and give evidence of a return on your investment. Without this, the organization is misspending valuable resources. The management axiom that it is not managed unless it is measured applies here. This gives management quantifiable measurement tools to evaluate the performance of their marketing programs and sales channels.

The lead fulfillment process is one example of how these measurement tools are used. The effectiveness of your ability to satisfy a lead is measured by the percentage of information that actually gets to the prospect, and the prospect's willingness to keep it and access it. If the prospect does not receive it, or he or she is not willing to keep it and able to access it, then the information is of little value.

It should be noted that "closing the loop" through tracking all qualified leads may not be economically justified. Often, sampling qualified leads activity in the field is more appropriate. For example, inquirers are randomly contacted after they have been sent literature. The key measurements are retention and deliverability. If, when contacted, the inquirer recalls receiving the information, that satisfies the deliverability measurement. If they can access the information that was delivered, that satisfies the retention measurement. These measurements give management a means of monitoring the effectiveness of the inquiry handling process.

The two most important measures of lead management are: (1) cost/qualified lead (by individual lead source), and (2) sales closure/qualified lead (by sales rep, office, district, region, etc.). Both depend on the "qualified lead" as a primary measure of potential value.

Acquisition and cultivation have to be approached as two separate processes. You simply cannot effectively measure the processes in acquisition and compare that to the processes in cultivation or retention because the economics are so radically different.

NEW CUSTOMER ASSIMILATION

Assimilation is the process of absorbing customers into your culture—building a "community of customers." You want to bond with the new customer, take this new customer into your mind, and thoroughly comprehend what they're about. You also want to improve the customer's perception and understanding of the kind of relationship they could have with you.

The first step is to learn as much as possible about the new customer. This starts with a phone call, which is the most important phone call you can make—the first phone call to a customer following receipt of the product/service. This starts the process of assimilation and begins to establish your new relationship with the customer. This transition from event focus (lead, qualified lead, demo, sale) to a relationship is difficult. It requires planning, new people on your team, and a well-disciplined contact program.

You start by thanking them for their order and asking if they had any problems. Then you begin profiling the customer. You want to find out how they want to be contacted about certain types of information. You need to listen with intensity to what their needs and concerns are. This information is immediately placed in the database to be used in future contacts.

A helpful way to approach this initial assimilation planning is to write down how you welcome new employees into your organization. Or, write down the meaningful ways in which you have been assimilated into a new neighborhood, church, or some other organization. These are the same types of contacts that should be built into a new customer assimilation program.

From this, you can create a value-based communication contact plan. You should grade new customers just as you graded existing customers. You should predict revenue streams and develop a program that meets the anticipated revenue stream. The same people within the organization who handle account management should handle assimilation. This makes for a seamless transition for a new customer into the customer community.

As part of the assimilation process, you investigate other opportunities within the customer's organization. You apply the same penetration strategies used for increasing business with current customers. That is, use the account cube model in Chapter 7 and locate other areas within the new customer's location, group, and organization for new business. Once again, you are leveraging the relationship with current customers. Remember, loyalty is built on the four basics of recency, frequency, monetary amount, and referrals. If you can increase the number of buyers per location and the number of product lines purchased per location, you are building a loyal customer.

Keep in mind, you invested in new customer acquisition based on the anticipated revenue stream. In order to realize that revenue stream, you need to retain these new customers. This is especially important during the early stages of the budding relationship.

It is also during this assimilation process you determine if the new customer is one you want to retain. For example, if you find during the assimilation process the customer is chronically late on paying invoices, demands excessive service, or exhibits other uncivil behavior, you may want to discourage that customer from repurchasing or certainly limit the resources used to support their needs.

Frederick Reichheld of Bain & Company commented on this, "With knowledge of which customers are likely to be loyal comes knowledge of which customers are not. Companies can then direct resources away from customers who are unlikely to stay."[10]

During assimilation you also need to determine why the customer is buying from you and then build the relationship from a position of strength. The reasons a customer buys become potential external service values. The unfulfilled needs you satisfy become your strategic advantage with the customer.

Some companies are reluctant to undertake an assimilation program. They simply dump new customers into the existing customer base and trust these customers will understand the scope and limitations of the relationship. If you have any doubts about the value of assimilation, set up a test and control group. As you acquire new customers, assign the customers to the test group or to the control group. With the test group, you follow the principles of customer assimilation. The control group does not receive this treatment. Then you measure life-to-date revenues from each group on a monthly basis. The differences will be significant and the results will graphically show the importance of assimilation.

THE BUSINESS-TO-BUSINESS RELATIONSHIP CYCLE

Through the previous chapters, the steps have been documented for building a customer community through developing sustainable relationships with the customer that lead to loyalty and community. The major elements of this process are summarized in Figure 8-6.

When one follows these steps, one can begin developing a sense of community with customers. This is predicated on building a positive interdependence between you and the customer. Through this, you build a solid customer base resistant to competitive pressures, provided you maintain the necessary core competencies to satisfy customer needs. You become sensitive to a customer's changing needs and take the steps to nurture the relationship.

Phase	Description	Needs	Destructive Action
Lead Generation	• Getting noticed • Generating a response	• Must have a need • Offer must fit • Must be interested • Expectations must align	• Wrong target • Not addressing needs • Focusing on own needs • Overpromising • Excessive nonvalue-based contacts • Misrepresenting
Prospect Cultivation	• Developing deeper relationships prior to making a commitment	• Increased knowledge • Reduced uncertainty • Understanding the potential benefit • Seeing a win/win	• Indifference • Superficial contact • Mixed messages • Prescribing before diagnosing • Not addressing needs • Focusing on own needs
First Sale	• First major commitment		
Assimilation	• Becoming comfortable with, and committing to, a long-term relationship	• Affirmation • Feeling valued • Treated like an "insider" • Increased involvement	• Indifference • Not acknowledging the relationship • Not expressing appreciation • Not reinforcing the decision • Not encouraging a second purchase • Acquiring the wrong customers in the first place
Product Penetration	• Strengthening the individual relationship by delivering increasing value with additional products and services • Functionally similar to assimilation	• Deeper understanding of business needs • Proactivity • Added value • Value-based contacts • Empathy	• Indifference • Treating customers and prospects the same way • Not being proactive • Superficial contact • Mixed messages

Stage		Needs	Pitfalls
		• Frequent contact • Trust and confidence • Interdependency • Mutual benefit	• Prescribing before diagnosing • Not addressing needs • Focusing on own needs • Focusing on the transaction • Focusing on single lines
Account Penetration	• Strengthening the overall relationship by selling products and services to new individuals inside of existing accounts • Functionally similar to lead generation	• Must have a need • Offer must fit • Must be interested • Expectations must align	• Not leveraging the existing corporate relationship • Wrong target • Not addressing needs • Focusing on own needs • Overpromising • Misrepresenting
Reactivation	• Activating a dormant or declining customer • Winning back defected customers	• Feeling valued • Proactivity • Value-based contacts • Empathy • Trust and confidence	• Indifference • Not acknowledging the prior relationship • Not expressing appreciation • Not being proactive • Prescribing before diagnosing • Focusing on own needs • Focusing on the transaction
Damage Control	• Taking immediate and appropriate action to retain the relationship • Damage control can occur at any stage of a customer's lifecycle	• To easily complain • To receive a quick and appropriate response • An apology • To be listened to • To be valued • To be treated fairly and justly	• Indifference • Not responding with urgency • Providing a solution before listening • Rationalizing • Insincerity • Not focusing on the long-term consequences

Figure 8-6 Business-to-Business Relationship Process

© Hunter Business Direct, Inc.

Companies that do not get close to their customers will not survive the next decade of business-to-business marketing. There are no choices. Either change or lose your market position. Unfortunately, the landscape over the next ten years will be littered with companies who believed they had all the answers and failed to listen to their customers. Today's competitive advantage will become tomorrow's devastation if the principles of customer community are not followed.

COMMUNITY BUILDING IN ACTION: BUSINESSFORMS

For the BusinessForms division, an acquisition strategy encompassed several sources for new business. The first avenue they wanted to explore was establishing an alliance with a dental supplier, similar to the alliances they had formed with accounting software publishers and VARs. So they analyzed who sold to dentists and formed an alliance with a major supplier of plastic materials used in dentistry.

This alliance provided the division with a comprehensive list of contacts at dental offices. However, rather than contact all dentists, the division now looked at their current customer base and began developing a set of criteria to use in targeting prospects. For example, one requirement was that the dentist's practice be at least $400,000 annually.

Those dentists that did not meet this requirement would be added to the existing list for this segment and would receive regular mailings with no telephone follow-up or face-to-face contact. This would be a reactive situation in which the division would react to an inquiry but not invest in furthering the relationship.

Once the target list was developed, the division next compared that list with their existing customer base. They purged current customers from the list and looked for duplicated addresses, etc.

The next step was to develop a message or offer. This was accomplished by examining the external service values of their current customers. For example, for a dentist who was a satellite office of a large group, the external service value of maintaining the integrity of graphics had proved to be important. So, the offer to this group or segment would include that information.

The division also had other avenues to explore. Trade shows were a potential source of new business leads. Also, the division began developing relationships with dental schools and contacted newly graduated dentists with a package that helped them get started with the forms they needed in a practice. By developing a relationship with the dental schools, the division was able to be in contact with the dental authorities associated with the school that had influence among the dental community.

In every step the division took toward acquiring new business, they continually evaluated the names on lists to ensure the list attributes matched the attributes of their best current customers.

Notes

1. Frederick F. Reichheld, "Loyalty-Based Management," *Harvard Business Review,* March–April 1993, 65–66.

2. Gary J. Coles and James D. Culley, "Not All Prospects Are Created Equal," *Business Marketing,* May 1986, 57.

3. Bob Stone, *Successful Direct Marketing Methods,* 5th ed. (Lincolnwood, IL: NTC Business Books, 1994), 77.

4. *Commercial Sites Index Weekly Summary* (4 April 1996). Available at: http://www.directory.net/dir/statistics.html

5. "GE Plastics Takes the Internet Plunge," *Business Week,* 24 October 1994. (See GE Plastics at URL: http://www.ge.com/GEPlastics/homepage.html)

6. Herbert E. Brown and Roger W. Brucker, "Telephone Qualification of Sales Leads," *Industrial Marketing Management* 16, 1987, 185.

7. Ibid.

8. Rowland T. Moriarty and Gordon S. Swartz, "Automation to Boost Sales and Marketing," *Harvard Business Review,* January–February 1989, 103.

9. * Win_News, maintained by the Microsoft Personal Operating Systems Division to distribute information on Windows, MS-DOS, and Windows "Chicago." Available at: http://www.microsoft.com/chicago/ms-www/ms-intro.html

10. Reichheld, 66–67.

9

LEADERSHIP AND THE NEW CUSTOMER COMMUNITY

This book began with a reference to the memorable United Airlines television ad. It's based on a "remarkably new idea" that is as old as business itself: Success in business depends on treating your customer as an individual.

Getting close to the customer has become the rallying cry of the '90s. From integrated marketing communications to one-to-one marketing and beyond, it has received much attention in the business press and other publications. Companies adopting early versions of this "born again" devotion to customers have had mixed results, in either their ability to build stronger relationships with their customers or in their ability to do so profitably.

The reasons that few have been successful are varied. First, in order to build stronger customer relationships you need to overcome cultural roadblocks that prevent the organization from treating the customer as an individual rather than an account or "piece of business." Second, unless you are able to economically measure and act on the results generated through building relationships you will not sustain profitability.

"Creating a Community of Customers"—the subtitle of this book—addresses these issues in a new way that marries business relationships with economic well-being and prosperity in a community of shared interests and values, with mutual (interdependent) concerns and objectives. This chapter summarizes the basic concepts that will start you on the journey to building a community of customers.

In many ways, the journey metaphor is appropriate for community building. This is not a quick fix. Rather it requires a fundamental change in the way a company conducts its business. Consider this basic business principle: businesses typically are not formed with the intent of being operational for a specific period of time. The majority of business enterprises, while they may undergo change, expect to be operational for an infinite period of time. The same then should hold true for customers, i.e., a company should expect customer relationships to last generation after generation if they are, in fact, the lowest cost source of revenues over time and provide high value to the customer. This being the case, then building a community of customers, and sustaining that community, becomes a life-long process, or journey.

This is basic to understanding the concept of the customer community. If you start thinking about customers as being lifetime partners, then you move away from the traditional transaction-based approach (short-term/quick fix) to marketing and sales, which emphasizes getting the order rather than keeping the customer. You start to think in terms of generations of customers. Which means you have to understand your customer's needs and deliver economic value to them in order to sustain that relationship.

THE BASICS OF CUSTOMER COMMUNITY

Community is both a place and a state of mind. The place part of community is like a neighborhood. It is the physical part of community and includes such things as frequent transactions and proximity. The state of mind is more elusive. It is not a constant. You continually go into and out of a state of community. But, you need a commitment to community as a vision or goal to continually strive for. This commitment hinges on economics, integrity, service, balance, personal encouragement, and a shared understanding of community.

Let's look at the customer community process as outlined in this book. It has focused on the journey as a means of understanding how to form a covenant with your customer. To review, the basics in this journey include:

- Recognize that it is a real person within the account or organization who is the buyer, influencer, decision maker, specifier, etc., of your product or service.

- Gather information about customers through repeated contacts with them, using direct mail, telephone, and face-to-face contacts.

- Identify shared values, i.e., external service values, from this information.

- Develop a communication and contact plan that delivers value at every point of contact with the individual.

- Cultivate the customer, which leads to building the relationship.

COMMUNITY LEADERSHIP—STARTING FROM WITHIN

Before one can build a sense and spirit of community with the customer, the same must be evident within the organization. You cannot attempt to create this customer community and build long-term relationships if you have a short-term "take advantage of the employee" attitude internally. First, you must build community within your company and yourself. Your culture, attitudes, values, and the way you treat each other are going to extend to the customer.

William Davidow and Bro Uttal, authors of *Total Customer Satisfaction,* observed, "Becoming a service leader takes more than good general management. It calls for making profound changes in the way you operate. It often requires building a new, service-oriented culture. The task is daunting for effective companies and impossible for ones that are foundering."[1]

For a customer community to exist and flourish, a customer focus must be woven as a common thread through the entire organization. Culture is comprised of the norms, values, and beliefs shared by members of the organization. These are directly influenced by the organization's leadership. The ability of an organization to pursue a goal of customer community is dependent upon the leadership of the organization.

This community of customers requires a new style of leadership, which is often referred to as servant-leadership. Larry Spears, executive director of the Robert K. Greenleaf Center for Servant-Leadership described this as: "Traditional modes of leadership are slowly yielding to a new model—one which is based upon teamwork and community. It seeks to involve others in decision-making, is based on ethical behavior, and attempts to enhance the personal growth of workers while improving the caring and quality of our institutions. This emerging approach is called servant-leadership."[2]

Servant-leadership gained credibility in the 1980s as a leadership style that was stronger than classical management or administrative styles. This is a style built around leadership and not around management techniques or administrative issues. Rather, it is about recognizing the humanness of the individual and empowering the individual. In this style of leadership, the top executive does not lead people, whether employees or customers, but rather serves them by helping them understand how they can grow to be the best that they can be.

Tim Hoeksema, founding president of Midwest Express airline, practices servant-leadership. The airline, which began in 1984 out of Kimberly-Clark Corp.'s corporate aviation division, is considered one of the nation's best regional carriers. Hoeksema explained, "My job is to support my deputies and everyone else—to listen, respond and give them what they need to get the job done. My job is to pitch in wherever I am needed."[3]

Without leadership, any attempt at building a customer community is doomed. Without a total commitment from top management, customer-focused programs cannot survive. Employee satisfaction and retention are highly correlated to customer satisfaction and retention.

EXPANDING TO A LARGER COMMUNITY

The type of customer community being described is the simple one-on-one spirit of community between the individual customer and yourself. But, obviously, community should embrace more than that. Typically, when one thinks of a community they envision a collection of individuals with a shared set of values and common objectives. And, as part of the community, there has to be the opportunity for interaction between members of the community. Through exchanging information, sharing value, and regularly interacting with one another, stronger community bonds are built.

One of the most difficult challenges in business-to-business marketing is taking ownership of the end user through forging healthy bonds with a channel partner, whether they are an independent sales representative, distributor, VAR, dealer, or other reseller. When a company is operating with a multichannel distribution system, getting close to the ultimate user of your product is of paramount concern. Only through understanding the end user are you able to determine external service values and unfulfilled needs to drive product development. Without this knowledge, both you and your channel partner can only be marginally competitive.

Of course, the first step in forging bonds with the channel partner is to build a spirit and sense of community with them. Much of this is dependent upon the trust each has for the other. Without mutual trust, community is not possible. For example, the manufacturer fulfills its role by building awareness of the product or service, by differentiating the product or service, and by educating the end user. However, when the manufacturer does these things, the channel partner may feel threatened. Therefore, in addition, the manufacturer needs to educate the channel partner and sponsor a shared understanding of the customer and the customer's needs. The shared understanding, and how best to meet the customer's needs, must drive the economics and behavior of both the manufacturer and the channel partner.

The manufacturer must create real value for the customer, as mentioned previously. This value then becomes an area in which the channel member is dependent upon the manufacturer. The manufacturer is dependent upon the channel member to take responsibility for servicing the customer and providing the type of service that best fits the segment's needs. Both form a shared interdependency with the customer.

When you have established a spirit of community with channel members and the interdependence that is an essential part of community, you have the opportunity to gain knowledge about the end user. A shared understanding between and with your channel partners is necessary in order to serve the end user competitively. Without this, you both are at a disadvantage. The sustainable business relationship must be built on serving the customer. The manufacturer needs the right channel member services and the channel partner needs the right manufacturer products and services. Sharing customer information is the foundation for serving the customer.

This enables us to change the dynamics of the relationship. Figure 9-1 shows the traditional linkage between internal and external entities compared with a community-oriented linkage.

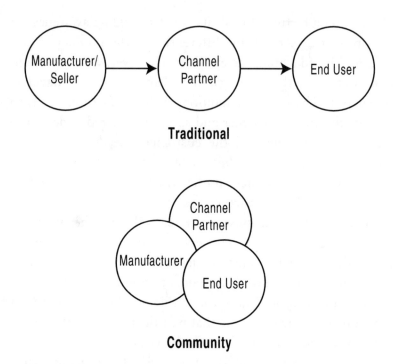

Figure 9-1 Traditional Versus Community Linkage

© Hunter Business Direct, Inc.

With traditional linkage, the manufacturer's internal community links with the channel partner, and the channel partner links with the end user. The manufacturer has limited, direct individual contact with the end user. The ideal community linkage is when the manufacturer not only links with the channel partner, but also touches the end user. The channel partner still has the major sphere of influence in the relationship with the end user, but the manufacturer now has contact with the customer community.

A RETURN TO INDIVIDUAL VALUES

Even with committed leadership, the success or failure of customer community relies to a great degree on the frontline customer contact person. They must share the values of the community concept and be attuned to the customer-focused culture. They operationalize the vision. This also means the individual must have a strong value structure and an appropriate behavioral profile, which translates to ethical behaviors and attitudes in the workplace.

Too often, a person takes a disassociated attitude into the customer relationship. This needs to change at the most basic level—within the person. The personal values that a person brings to the workplace must be consistent with the organization's cultural values. Matching the core values of the individual and organization is critical. It is only then that the person can begin the process of dealing with customers as individuals and not as impersonalized accounts.

A recent client situation, in which an employee was in a business environment that encouraged personal values, illustrates this. This involved a telemarketing representative who saw the volume of activity increase five-fold. When she raised the issue with management, the response was they understood her concerns, but the economics would not support additional resources.

In most organizations this would be the end of it. However, this was an organization that professed delivering quality service to the customer. So, the telemarketing representative bypassed the chain of command and proclaimed this was not an economic issue, but was an issue that struck at the core of the organization. If the company was committed to quality service, then she was not able to deliver it under existing conditions. Her actions caused management to reconsider the previous decision and resources were doubled to handle the increased customer activity. This is an example of personal integrity coming to the forefront.

THE JOURNEY TO COMMUNITY

Building a community of customers requires that you change the way in which you do business. You move from transactions to solutions, from getting the order to helping the customer. As demonstrated throughout this book, this is not an altruistic business approach, but one based on economic reality; loyal customers are more profitable and lead to additional revenues and profits.

This book is the starting point for your journey toward building a customer community. It is analogous to launching an expedition. It requires careful planning, ample resources, and a deep commitment. Just like an expedition, you don't do this alone. You need the support and involvement of the entire organization—from top management to field salespeople to everyone whose organizational role touches on the customer relationship.

Once you embark on this journey, you will find that this new "partnership" with the customer delivers substantial benefits. You will become smarter in the products or services you provide as they will be based on documented customer needs. You will have a more efficient organization as your processes will be driven from a customer's perspective. Processes that put customers at risk are changed. There will be a seamless appearance between the products/services you create, the requirements of your channel partners, and the needs of your ultimate user or customer. Your customers will become another sales channel as they take on the role of apostle for you. And, you will see revenues and profits grow.

You build this new customer community by:

- Listening at every point of customer contact so you can create value in the relationship

- Using integrity and encouragement to build relationships

- Providing servant-leadership that transforms the sales and marketing processes

- Having a balance that produces profitable growth through customer loyalty

- Sharing the spirit of your organization in a more civil and interdependent way of doing business

Building, sustaining, and growing a customer community is not a new business fad. Rather, it is a return to the fundamentals of sales and marketing that have been lost in the fascination with mass marketing and economics of transactions. It's a return to the one-on-one customer relationships that have proven to be the more sustainable way of doing business. Without a community approach, you are severely limiting your ability to survive as you move into the next century. This is the way business will be conducted. If you don't embrace it totally, you put your company at risk. This is a new spirit in the workplace. Join us on this journey to customer community.

Notes

1. William H. Davidow and Bro Uttal, *Total Customer Service: The Ultimate Weapon* (New York: Harper & Row, 1989), xix.

2. Http://www.umich.edu/~ballroom/ballroom-326.html

3. George Stanley, "Airline Chief Learned to Lead by Example," *Milwaukee Journal Sentinel,* 26 June 1995, 15D.

SELECTED READINGS

Abrams, Michael, and Matthew Paese. "Wining and Dining the Whiners." *Sales & Marketing Management,* February 1993, 73–75.

Akre, Brian S. "What Do We Like? ASQC Index Knows." *Milwaukee Journal,* 26 October 1994, C5.

Ames, Charles B., and James D. Hlavacek. *Market-Driven Management: Prescriptions for Survival in a Turbulent World.* Homewood, IL: Dow Jones-Irwin, 1989.

Appleton, Elaine L. "Bonding With Customers Through Better Service." *Datamation,* 1 November 1993, 69–72.

Baker, Susan. "Digital Zeroes In." *Business Marketing,* November 1991, 60–62.

Barnard, David C. "Integrating an In-House Center." *Direct Marketing,* December 1988, 72–75.

Bauer, Connie L., and John Miglautsch. "A Conceptual Definition of Direct Marketing." *Journal of Direct Marketing* 6:2 (Spring 1992), 7–17.

Bencin, Richard L. "The Trouble with (Some) Telemarketers." *Business Marketing,* August 1986, 80–83.

Berling, Robert J. "The Emerging Approach to Business Strategy: Building a Relationship Advantage." *Business Horizons,* July–August 1993, 16–27.

Berry, Jonathan. "Database Marketing: A Potent New Tool For Selling." *Business Week,* 5 September 1994, 56–62.

Berry, Leonard L., and A. Parasuraman. "Prescriptions For a Service Quality Revolution in America." *Organizational Dynamics,* Spring 1992, 5–15.

Berry, Leonard L., Valarie A. Zeitbaml, and A. Parasuraman. "Five Imperatives For Improving Service Quality." *Sloan Management Review,* Summer 1990, 29–38.

Bertrand, Kate. "A Potent Combination." *Business Marketing,* November 1991, 58.

Blattberg, Robert C., and John Deighton. "Interactive Marketing: Exploiting the Age of Addressability." *Sloan Management Review,* Fall 1991, 5–14.

Blattberg, Robert C., Rashi Glazer, and John D. C. Little, eds. *The Marketing Information Revolution.* Boston: Harvard Business School Press, 1994.

Brown, Herbert E., and Roger W. Brucker. "Telephone Qualification of Sales Leads." *Industrial Marketing Management* 16 (1987), 185–190.

Brown, Priscilla C. "No Quick Fix." *Business Marketing,* September 1992, 91, 98.

Burns, Greg. "Will So Many Ingredients Work Together?" *Business Week,* 27 March 1995, 188.

Byers, C. R., and L. J. Morris. "Enhancing Sales Force Productivity With a Relational DBMS." *Journal of Systems Management,* January 1991, 13–17.

Byrne, John A. "The Pain of Downsizing." *Business Week,* 9 May 1994, 34.

Byrne, John A. "Why Downsizing Looks Different These Days." *Business Week,* 10 October 1994, 43.

Cannie, Joan Koob. *Turning Lost Customers Into Gold: . . . and the Art of Achieving Zero Defections.* New York: Amacon, 1994.

Cespedes, Frank V. *Concurrent Marketing: Integrating Product, Sales, and Service.* Boston: Harvard Business School Press, 1995.

Chandler, Colby H. "Beyond Customer Satisfaction." *Quality Progress,* February 1989, 30.

Chase, Richard B., and David A. Garvin. "The Service Factory." *Harvard Business Review,* July–August 1989, 61–62.

Christopher, Martin, Adrian Payne, and David Ballantyne. *Relationship Marketing: Bringing Quality, Customer Service, and Marketing Together.* Oxford (UK): Butterworth Heinemann, 1991.

Clancy, Kevin J. "The Dangers of Death-Wish Marketing." *Planning Review,* September–October 1992, 53–55.

Clarke, Peter A., and David Murray. "Information Technology in Customer Service." *Business Quarterly,* Spring 1990, 91–94.

Coles, Gary J., and James D. Culley. "Not All Prospects Are Created Equal." *Business Marketing,* May 1986, 52–58.

Conlon, Grace. "Turning Database Support Into Success." *Marketing Communications,* June 1986, 90–95.

Copp, Vincent F. "Reinventing Direct Marketing." *Journal of Direct Marketing,* Autumn 1989, 16–27.

Coppett, John, and Roy Dale Voorhees. "Telemarketing: A New Weapon in the Arsenal." *Journal of Business Strategy,* Spring 1983, 80–83.

Coppett, John I., and Roy Dale Voorhees. "Telemarketing: Supplement to Field Sales." *Industrial Marketing Management* 14 (1985), 213–216.

Cortada, James W. *TQM for Sales and Marketing Management.* New York: McGraw-Hill, 1993.

Cosco, Joseph. "The Razor's Edge." *The Journal of Business Strategy,* November/December 1993, 58–61.

Covey, Stephen R. *The 7 Habits of Highly Effective People.* New York: Simon and Schuster, 1989.

"Creating Customer Loyalty." *Management Solutions,* January 1988, 28.

Cross, Richard, and Janet A. Smith. "New Product Launches." *Direct Marketing,* August 1992, 35–41.

Dallaire, Rene M. "Data-Based Marketing for Competitive Advantage." *Information Strategy,* Spring 1992, 5–9.

Damian, Jacqueline. "Does Your Company Pass Or Fail Service?" *Electronics,* May 1991, 48–56.

"Database Marketing Demystified." *Target Marketing,* June 1993, 13.

Davidow, William H., and Bro Uttal. "Service Companies: Focus or Falter." *Harvard Business Review,* July–August 1989, 77–85.

Davidow, William H., and Bro Uttal. *Total Customer Service: The Ultimate Weapon.* New York: Harper & Row, 1989.

Davidow, William H., and Michael S. Malone. *The Virtual Corporation: Structuring and Revitalizing the Corporation for the 21st Century.* New York: HarperCollins, 1992.

De Rose, Louis J. "How Industrial Markets Buy Value Selling: A Strategy for Dealing with Changes. *The Journal of Business and Industrial Marketing,* Winter 1992, 65–69.

Deeprose, Donna. "Helping Employees Handle Difficult Customers." *Supervisory Management,* September 1991, 6.

Dent Jr., Harry S. "Individualized Marketing: Using Databases to Build One-On-One Customer Relationships." *Small Business Reports,* April 1991, 36–37.

Derks, Richard P. "Business Trends: Data Base Marketing." *Information Strategy,* Winter 1994, 34–37.

DeSouza, Glenn. "Designing a Customer Retention Plan." *The Journal of Business Strategy,* March/April 1992, 24–28.

Duncan III, R. C. (Rusty). "The Company with the Most Info Wins." *Industrial Distribution,* February 1993, 52.

Dwyer, F. Robert, Paul H. Schurr, and Sejo Oh. "Developing Buyer-Seller Relationships." *Journal of Marketing,* April 1987, 11–27.

Eisenhart, Tom. "An Interplay of Information." *Business Marketing,* September 1992, 90–92.

Eisenhart, Tom. "Dell, Polaroid Use Databases to Target Customers, Link Internal Units." *Business Marketing,* May 1992, 24–26.

Eisenhart, Tom. "GE's 'Relational Database' Keeps Lines Open to Customers." *Business Marketing,* May 1992, 27.

Eisenhart, Tom. "Telemarketing Takes Quantum Leap." *Business Marketing,* September 1993, 75–76.

Etherington, Bill. "Putting Customer Satisfaction to Work." *Business Quarterly,* Summer 1992, 128–131.

"Field Sales Automation: Where Outside Meets Inside." *Telemarketing,* March 1992, 64–68.

Flanagan, Theresa A., and Joan O. Fredericks. "Improving Company Performance Through Customer-Satisfaction Measurement and Management." *National Productivity Review,* Spring 1993, 239–258.

Fletcher, Keith, Colin Wheeler, and Julia Wright. "Strategic Implementation of Database Marketing: Problems and Pitfalls." *Long Range Planning* 27, February 1994, 133–141.

Flint, Jerry with William Heuslein. "An Urge to Service." *Forbes,* 18 September 1989, 172–176.

Fornell, Claes, and Birger Wernerfelt. "Defensive Marketing Strategy by Customer Complaint Management: A Theoretical Analysis." *Journal of Marketing Research,* November 1987, 337–346.

Fornell, Claes. "A National Customer Satisfaction Barometer: The Swedish Experience." *Journal of Marketing,* January 1992, 6–21.

Galen, Michelle. "Companies Hit the Road Less Traveled." *Business Marketing,* 5 June 1995, 82.

"GE Plastics Takes the Internet Plunge." *Business Week,* 24 October 1994, 93.

Ginsburg, Dan. "Business-to-Business in 1990: How to Get Ready for Change." *Direct Marketing,* March 1985, 24–32.

Gleckman, Howard. "A Tonic for the Business Cycle." *Business Week,* 4 Apr 1994, 57ff.

Goldberg, Bernard. "Relationship Marketing." *Direct Marketing,* October 1988, 103–105.

Goodkin, Michael J. "Relationship Marketing, Multi-Channel Distribution, and Databases: New Needs in the Classroom and Opportunities for Research." *Journal of Direct Marketing,* 5:3 (Summer 1991), 2–4.

Goodman, John A., Elizabeth A. Brigham, and Rick Cottrell. "Turning Customers' Complaints into a Marketing Asset." *Electric Perspectives,* Fall 1988, 32–37.

Goodman, John, Scott M. Broetzmann, and Dianne S. Ward. "Preventing TQM Problems: Measured Steps Toward Customer-Driven Quality Improvement." *National Productivity Review,* Autumn 1993, 555–571.

Goodman, John. "The Nature of Customer Satisfaction." *Quality Progress,* February 1989, 37–40.

Gouillart, Francis J., and Frederick D. Sturdivant. "Spend a Day in the Life of Your Customers." *Harvard Business Review,* January–February 1994, 116–125.

Greenberg, Marshall, and Susan Schwartz McDonald. "Successful Needs/Benefits Segmentation: A User's Guide." *The Journal of Consumer Marketing,* Summer 1989, 29–36.

Greising, David. "Watch Out for Flying Packages." *Business Week,* 14 November 1994, 40.

Gronroos, Christian. "Relationship Approach to Marketing in Service Contexts: The Marketing and Organizational Behavior Interface." *The Journal of Business Research* 20 (1990), 3–11.

Hammer, Michael, and James Champy. *Reengineering the Corporation: A Manifesto for Business Revolution.* New York: HarperCollins, 1993.

Hansotia, Behram. "List Segmentation: How to Find Your Best Direct Marketing Prospects." *Business Week,* August 1986, 64–76.

Harari, Oren. "Thank Heaven for Complainers." *Management Review,* January 1992, 59–60.

Harlan, Raymond, and Walter Woolfson, Jr. *Telemarketing That Works: How to Create a Winning Program for Your Company.* Chicago: Probus 1991.

Hart, Christopher W. L., James L. Heskett, and W. Earl Sasser, Jr. "The Profitable Art of Service Recovery." *Harvard Business Review,* July–August 1990, 148–156.

Heard, Ed. "Walking the Talk of Customer Service." *National Productivity Review,* Winter 1993/94, 21–27.

Hensler, D. Jack. "The Customer Satisfaction Link to TQM." *National Productivity Review,* Spring 1994, 165.

Herrington, Mike. "What Does a Customer Want?" *Across the Board,* April 1993, 33–35.

Heskett, James L., Thomas O. Jones, Gary W. Loveman, W. Earl Sasser, Jr., and Leonard Schlesinger. "Putting the Service-Profit Chain to Work." *Harvard Business Review,* March–April 1994, 164–174.

Ives, Blake, and Richard O. Mason. "Can Information Technology Revitalize Your Customer Service?" *Academy of Management Executive* 4:4 (1990), 52–69.

Jacob, Rahul. "Beyond Quality and Value" *Fortune,* Autumn/Winter 1993, 8–11.

Jacob, Rahul. "Why Some Customers Are More Equal Than Others." *Fortune,* 12 September 1994, 215–224.

Kauffman, Ronald S. *Future$ell: Automating Your Sales Force.* Boulder, CO: Cross Communications Company, 1990.

Keefe, Mark. "Letting the Right Hand Know What the Left Hand Is Doing." *Direct Marketing,* July 1993, 18–20.

Kiechel III, Walter. "Corporate Strategy for the 1990s." *Fortune,* 29 February 1988, 34.

Kordupleski, Raymond E. "How Good Do You Have To Be?" *Across the Board,* May 1993, 47.

"Kotler Foresees Integrated Future." *Business Marketing,* September 1993, 85.

Kotler, Philip. "Marketing's New Paradigm: What's Really Happening Out There." *Planning Review,* September–October 1992, 50–52.

Kotler, Philip. *Marketing Management: Analysis, Planning, Implementation, and Control.* 6th ed. Englewood Cliffs, NJ: Prentice Hall, 1988.

Levitt, Theodore. "Marketing Success Through Differentiation—of Anything." *Harvard Business Review,* January–February 1980, 83–91.

Lukovitz, Karlene. "Get Ready for One-on-One Marketing." *Folio,* October 1991, 64–70.

Marshall, Judith J., and Harrie Vredenburg. "Successfully Using Telemarketing in Industrial Sales." *Industrial Marketing Management* 17 (1988), 15–22.

Marshall, Judith J., and Harrie Vredenburg. "The Roles of Outside and Inside Sales Representatives: Conflict or Cooperation?" *Journal of Direct Marketing* 5:4 (Autumn 1991), 8–17.

Martin, Justin. "Ignore Your Customer." *Fortune,* 1 May 1995, 121–126.

Maslow, Abraham H. *Eupsychian Management: A Journal.* Homewood, IL: Richard D. Irwin, Inc., and the Dorsey Press, 1965.

McGaughey, Nick. "Customer Service: Lessons From World-Class Companies." *Industrial Engineering,* March 1993, 18–20.

McKenna, Regis. *Relationship Marketing: Successful Strategies for the Age of the Customer*. Reading, Mass.: Addison-Wesley, 1991.

McLeod, Jonah. "The Godfather Program." *Electronics,* May 1991, 54.

Miglautsch, John. "The Great Database Myth Is Dead!!!" *Direct Marketing,* June 1992, 23–25.

Moncrief III, William C., Charles W. Lamb, Jr., and Jane M. Mackay. "Laptop Computers in Industrial Sales." *Industrial Marketing Management* 20 (1991), 279–285.

Moncrief, William C., Charles W. Lamb, Jr., and Terry Dielman. "Developing Telemarketing Support Systems." *Journal of Personal Selling & Sales Management,* August 1986, 43–49.

Moriarty, Rowland T., and Gordon S. Swartz. "Automation to Boost Sales and Marketing." *Harvard Business Review,* January–February 1989, 100–108.

Morris, David. "What's Old Is New in Relationship Marketing." *Marketing News,* 14 February 1994, 4ff.

Narus, James A., and James C. Anderson. "Industrial Selling: The Roles of Outside and Inside Sales." *Industrial Marketing Management* 15 (1986), 55–62.

Noel, James L., Dave Ulrich, and Steven R. Mercer. "Customer Education: A New Frontier for Human Resource Development." *Human Resource Management* 29:4 (Winter 1990), 411–34.

Normann, Richard, and Rafael Ramirez. "From the Value Chain to Value Constellation: Designing Interactive Strategy." *Harvard Business Review,* July–August 1993, 65–77.

O'Neal, Charles R. "JIT Procurement and Relationship Marketing." *Industrial Marketing Management* 18 (1989), 55–63.

Oetting, Rudy, and Geri Gantman. "Dial 'M' for Maximize." *Sales & Marketing Management,* June 1991, 100–106.

Oliva, Terence A., Richard L. Oliver, and Ian C. MacMillan. "A Catastrophe Model for Developing Service Satisfaction Strategies." *Journal of Marketing,* July 1992, 83–95.

"Opportunity Returns." *Dimensions,* Fall 1994, 16.

Pare, Terence P. "How to Find Out What They Want." *Fortune,* Autumn/Winter 1993, 39–41.

Perkins, W. Steven. "Measuring Customer Satisfaction: A Comparison of Buyer, Distributor, and Salesforce Perception of Competing Products." *Industrial Marketing Management* 22 (1993), 247–254.

Pesmen, Sandra. "Direct Mail Campaign Helps Videojet Get Back into 'Black Ink'." *Business Marketing,* November 1991, 58–59.

Peters, Tom. "The Tom Peters Seminar: Crazy Times Call for Crazy Organizations." New York: Vintage Books, 1994.

Petrison, Lisa A., and Paul Wang. "Relationship Issues in Creating the Customer Database: The Potential for Interdepartmental Conflict Between Marketing and MIS." *Journal of Direct Marketing* 7:4 (Autumn 1993), 54–62.

Petrison, Lisa A., Robert C. Blattberg, and Paul Wang. "Database Marketing: Past, Present, and Future." *Journal of Direct Marketing* 7:3 (Summer 1991), 27–43.

Power, Christopher. "How to Get Closer to Your Customers." *Business Week,* Special Enterprise Issue 1993, 42.

Rangan, V. Kasturi, Rowland T. Moriarty, and Gordon S. Swartz. "Segmenting Customers in Mature Industrial Markets." *Journal of Marketing,* October 1992, 72–82.

Rapp, Stan, and Thomas L. Collins. *Beyond MaxiMarketing: The New Power of Caring and Daring.* New York: McGraw-Hill, 1994.

Rapp, Stan, and Thomas L. Collins. *MaxiMarketing: The New Direction in Advertising, Promotion, and Marketing Strategy.* New York: McGraw-Hill, 1987.

Reichheld, Frederick F. "Loyalty-Based Management." *Harvard Business Review,* March–April 1993, 64–73.

Reichheld, Frederick F., and W. Earl Sasser, Jr. "Zero Defections: Quality Comes to Services." *Harvard Business Review,* September–October 1990, 105–111.

Richard, James G. "Increased Customer Service Begins in the Engineering Department." *Industrial Engineering,* August 1993, 61–62.

Roberts, Mary Lou. "Expanding the Role of the Direct Marketing Database." *Journal of Direct Marketing* 6:2 (Spring 1992), 51–60.

Rock, Andrea. "DuPont's New Fax Attack Moving on Several Fronts." *Business Marketing,* May 1992, 32–33.

Roman, Ernan. *Integrated Direct Marketing.* New York: McGraw-Hill, 1988.

Sager, Ira. "IBM Knows What to Do with a Good Idea: Sell It." *Business Week,* 19 September 1994, 72.

Sager, Ira. "The Few, the True, the Blue: IBM is Remaking Its Sales Force into a Whole New Machine." *Business Week,* 30 May 1994, 124–126.

Schlesinger, Leonard A., and Jeffrey Zornitsky. "Job Satisfaction, Service Capability, and Customer Satisfaction: An Examination of Linkages and Management Implications." *Human Resource Planning* 14:2 (1991), 141–149.

Schonberger, Richard J. *Building a Chain of Customers: Linking Business Functions to Create the World Class Company.* New York: The Free Press, 1990.

Schultz, Don E. "Will Direct Marketing Change Communication Theory?" *Journal of Direct Marketing* 6:2 (Spring 1992), 4–6.

Schultz, Don E. *Strategic Advertising Campaigns.* 3rd ed. Lincolnwood, IL: NTC Business Books, 1990.

Schwartz, Joe. "Databases Deliver the Goods." *American Demographics,* September 1989, 23–25ff.

Sellers, Patricia. "How to Handle Customers' Gripes." *Fortune,* 24 October 1988, 88–100.

Sellers, Patricia. "Keeping the Buyers You Already Have." *Fortune,* Autumn/Winter 1993, 56–58.

Sellers, Patricia. "What Customers Really Want." *Fortune,* 4 June 1990, 58–68.

Shandle, Jack. "Learning How to Listen." *Electronics,* May 1991, 49.

Sherman, Strafford. "How to Prosper in the Value Decade." *Fortune,* 30 November 1992, 90–103.

Sinha, Madhav N. "Winning Back Angry Customers." *Quality Progress,* November 1993, 53.

Stanley, George. "Airline Chief Learned to Lead by Example." *Milwaukee Journal Sentinel,* 26 June 1995, 15D.

Stone, Bob. *Successful Direct Marketing Methods.* 5th ed. Lincolnwood, IL: NTC Business Books 1994.

"Strategy and the Art Of Reinventing Value." *Harvard Business Review,* September–October 1993, 39–51.

Sullivan, R. Lee. "The Office That Never Closes." *Forbes,* 23 May 1993, 212–213.

Taylor III, Alex. "GM's $11,000,000,000 Turnaround." *Fortune,* 17 October 1994, 56.

Taylor, Thayer C. "PCs Let Eaton Give Sweet Service." *Sales & Marketing Management,* October 1987, 91–92.

Tehrani, Nadji. "Integrated Marketing—The Wave of the Future." *Telemarketing,* June 1992, 2.

"There Are Not Products—Only Services." *Fortune,* 14 January 1991, 32.

Tinsley, Dillard B. "Management's Guide to an Integrated Marketing Strategy." *The Journal of Business Strategy,* November/December 1988, 30–33.

Tjosvold, Dean, Lindsay Meredith, and R. Michael Well-wood. "Implementing relationship marketing: A goal

interdependence approach." *Journal of Business &*
Industrial Marketing 8:4 (1993), 5–17.

Tornow, Walter W., and Jack W. Wiley. "Service Quality and
Management Practices: A Look at Employee Attitudes,
Customer Satisfaction, and Bottom-Line Consequences."
Human Resource Planning 14:2 (1991), 105–115.

Treacy, Michael, and Fred Wiersema. "Customer Intimacy
and Other Value Disciplines." *Harvard Business Review*,
January–February 1993, 84–93.

van Nievelt, M. C. Augustus. "Managing with Information
Technology—A Decade of Wasted Money?" *Information
Strategy*, Summer 1993, 5–17.

van Waterschoot, Walter, and Christophe Van den Bulte.
"The 4P Classification of the Marketing Mix Revisited."
Journal of Marketing, October 1992, 83–93.

VanHuss, Susie H. "Effective Customer Service." *Business
and Economic Review*, July–September 1993, 21–25.

Verity, John W. "Planet Internet: How the Center of the
Computer Universe Has Shifted." *Business Week*,
3 April 1995, 119–124.

Verity, John W. "The Internet: How It Will Change the Way
We Do Business." *Business Week*, 14 November 1994,
80–86.

Vivian, Barbara Tyler. "Qualifying Sales Leads." In *A
Growing Role for Business-to-Business Telemarketing*.
Ed. Earl L. Bailey. The Conference Board, Research
Report No. 912 (1988), 13–14.

Voorhees, Roy, and John Coppett. "Telemarketing in Distribution Channels." *Industrial Marketing Management* 12 (1983), 105–112.

Vredenburg, Harrie, and Judith Marshall. "A Field Experimental Investigation of a Social Influence Application in Industrial Marketing Communication Strategy." *Journal of Direct Marketing* 5:3 (Summer 1991), 7–8.

Wang, Paul. "Strategic Analysis and Choice: How Direct Marketers Can Succeed in the 1990s." *Journal of Direct Marketing* 6:2 (Spring 1992), 40–50.

Wayland, Robert E., and Paul M. Cole. "Turn Customer Service Into Customer Profitability." *Management Review,* July 1994, 22–24.

Weber, Samuel. "It's a Whole New Way of Doing Business." *Electronics,* July 1990, 54–58.

Welch, Mary. "Database Marketing Begins to Register." *Business Marketing,* March 1993, 48.

Whiting, Rick. "Customer Complaints Are an Untapped Source for Product Ideas." *Electronic Business,* July 1992, 7.

Wriston, Walter B. "Technology and Direct Marketing." *Vital Speeches of the Day* 55, 1 September 1989, 678.

Zibrun, Mike. "Relational Sales Training for the Competitive Edge." *Telemarketing,* September 1990, 68–71.